STOP AT NOTHING

STOP AT NOTHING ANNABEL CRABB

THE LIFE AND ADVENTURES OF MALCOLM TURNBULL

Black Inc.

Published by Black Inc.,
an imprint of Schwartz Publishing Pty Ltd
Level 1, 221 Drummond Street
Carlton VIC 3053, Australia
enquiries@blackincbooks.com
www.blackincbooks.com

National Library of Australia Cataloguing-in-Publication entry:
Crabb, Annabel, author.
Stop at nothing / Annabel Crabb.
9781863958189 (paperback)
9781925203943 (ebook)
Turnbull, Malcolm, 1954—
Liberal Party of Australia.
Politicians—Australia.
Prime ministers—Australia.
Australia—Politics and government—2001—
324.29405

Cover image by Louie Douvis
Cover design by Peter Long
Typesetting by Tristan Main

Printed in Australia by McPherson's Printing Group.

CONTENTS

When Bruce Turnbull died – horribly, shockingly, in a single-engine aircraft that speared to earth in dairy country on the mid north coast of New South Wales – it was a ghastly blow to his only son, Malcolm.

Bruce was fifty-six, and had just bought the beautiful Scone cattle farm of which he had dreamed his whole life. Malcolm was twenty-eight, with a newborn baby son.

The universe is fickle sometimes, but for Malcolm Turnbull – to whom it had given so parsimoniously in the family department – losing a father three months after gaining a son seemed dementedly, pointlessly cruel.

It smashed him up.

Bruce's affairs were tangled; properties here and there, and the farm itself was as dry as a twig, with a deep drought underway and urgent decisions to be made about stock, feed and other mysterious agrarian issues far from Turnbull's usual city life at the Sydney Bar.

In a crazy-brave manoeuvre, Turnbull kept the

farm. And he submerged his grief in – of all things –
the study of water.

"He had always been interested in Roman history ... aqueducts, and so on," recalls his wife, Lucy
Turnbull. "He totally immersed himself in the planning of bores and wells. It's really a classic example of
how he works."

In the absorbing detail of water tables, aquifers,
mineralisation and pipelines, Turnbull found respite
from the dragging anguish of bereavement. He loves
a knotty problem, and if it involves entering an arcane
world of complex widgetry and strange, beautiful
words (*alluvium*, *chelation*, *flocculation*, *capillarity*,
miscibility), then so much the better.

Even now, the science of water holds him in a
peculiarly tender way.

"I remember one day being here with [his son]
Al," he says one day when I am at the farm, filming
Kitchen Cabinet.

And it was pouring with rain and all the contour
banks were full of water and the dams were spilling
and the whole place was moving and the water was
moving everywhere and I took him and – he was
just a little boy, you know, with a hat and a little
Driza-Bone – and we went right up to the top of
that hill there and we just walked, we followed the

water all the way down and I reckon that was the best lesson you could ever give a boy about hydrology and water and landscape, because he actually saw how it worked. And then we got down to the bottom of that gully, where there is a well. Which is obviously tapping into the groundwater, and we looked down and I could show him the water moving through the groundwater, moving through the well, and come – you know – flowing into the well from the gravel and aggregate and sand and everything that's around it, so it was … ah, just so many memories like that. I love water.

The farm explains a lot about Malcolm Turnbull. Bruce is buried there, under a stone cairn. When he died, Malcolm kept everything. Bruce's hat. Bruce's boots. Even the stock that local cockies urged him to sell. He wore Bruce's watch for years.

But his mother, Coral, is there too. Coral walked out when Malcolm was eight, taking the furniture with her and running away with a new man, leaving her son and her husband in a bare flat. Malcolm was somehow allowed to believe that she was only gone for a while. It wasn't until he flew to visit her in New Zealand and was introduced – at the airport – to Coral's new fiancé that the penny dropped. And even then, Malcolm didn't resent her. He still doesn't, even though, in

Lucy's words, Coral continued to project "the most incredible expectations" onto her son, notwithstanding her personal absence.

Coral moved to Philadelphia with her new husband in the early 1970s. When, ten or so years later, the husband ran off with a graduate student, Turnbull hoped his mother would move back to Sydney. He bought a house for her in Paddington, which she never occupied, although she visited most years.

She died, in Philadelphia, of bowel cancer in 1991. And her son shipped everything home to Australia.

These days, the Scone farmhouse – beautifully renovated by Malcolm and Lucy – houses both Bruce's things and Coral's. All her books are there, and her furniture; even a hall table that still has – in a little drawer – the Philadelphia trolley-bus tokens she never got around to using.

It's an imperfect reunion; a pale simulacrum of the reconciliation the young Turnbull had hoped for very desperately. But whatever crumbs were left of his parents, he collected tenderly together in the end.

The trolley-bus tokens are heartbreaking, throat-grabbingly so; like watching one of those unbearable nature documentaries about grieving elephants touching their dead babies with their trunks. There's such an asymmetry of care involved: the child who treasures every scrap of his mother, the mother who squandered years with her son, continuing to demand extraordinary fealty from him despite having done just about everything imaginable to disqualify herself from any such expectation.

And the result: a complicated and fascinating person, who at sixty years of age became Australia's twenty-ninth prime minister. A man who has lost power, and gained it, and learnt from both experiences. A man widely known for his vaulting ambition and tooth-rattling tempers, who nevertheless brims with tears at the slightest provocation.

One night at dinner, Turnbull tells a story of how – not long after Coral left – Bruce took him swimming at North Bondi. Keen for a surf himself, Bruce gave a lifeguard a shilling to keep an eye on young Malcolm, who was barely nine. But the lifeguard lost interest, and Malcolm got into trouble. When Bruce made it back to shore, he couldn't see his son. "I remember going under ... I remember it so clearly, even today," Turnbull recalls. "I shouldn't tell this story, because even now it makes me so emotional." And it's true, there is a catch in his voice, and as he proceeds, Lucy monitors the situation with her customary cool vigilance.

"And to look up, finally, and see him – my father – coming for me, just powering through the waves ... I will never forget that feeling."

Hinterland

Something is missing in Australia. It's been missing since about 9.30 p.m. on 14 September 2015. On that day, one note – a deep, rich vibrato that has been a constant part of the rattling, tooting orchestral manoeuvre that is Australian politics for about forty years, sometimes building, sometimes ebbing, but always perceptibly there – abruptly stopped. Possibly forever.

What is this missing strain? It's the sound of Malcolm Bligh Turnbull wanting to be prime minister.

Up until that moment, Turnbull's was a life hugely defined by ambition. A life that began in modest circumstances, and was pierced early by maternal abandonment, but picked itself up and became – thanks to the efforts of its exuberant, brilliant, changeable occupant – extraordinary beyond the aspirations of all but the very few. It is a life that has surged through journalism and activism and business and politics, absorbing literature and art, and intersecting – sometimes happily, sometimes unhappily – with giants in those spheres.

It is a life that was given constancy and depth by marriage and children, but whose raw fuel was the urgent need to get somewhere, as fast as possible. The low hum of his ambition, all these years, has always been there in Australian public life; a composite note comprising countless Turnbull stories in which the protagonist makes millions, or pulls off some unbelievable legal coup, or goes to Siberia in search of gold, or picks a fight with a prime minister.

As Attorney-General George Brandis, a member of Malcolm Turnbull's leadership group, says, with lawyerly understatement: "Malcolm has more *hinterland* than any previous Australian prime minister."

A person who knows Turnbull very well told me that up until 2008, when he first became leader of the Liberal Party, his brain was occupied 50 per cent with whatever he was doing at the time, and 50 per cent by where he was going. After the loss of the leadership in 2009 – a miserable experience – that proportion receded to something more like 80/20; a moderation born of pain. And now that he's got what he and his mother wanted, he's achieved – in the estimation of his friend – something approaching peace.

A month or so into Turnbull's time as prime minister, he was telephoned by Alexander Downer. Presently Australia's high commissioner in London, Downer is a good friend of Turnbull's and the pair have a lot in common. They both ran unsuccessfully for Liberal pre-selection in 1981: Turnbull for Wentworth, Downer for the South Australian seat of Boothby.

Recalls Downer: "We both lost, and we commiserated with each other on the grounds that it was perfectly obvious that the worst candidates had won. We agreed that we were the stand-out talent, and the tragedy for the nation was that it would now have to wait for that which could quite easily have been its at an earlier date."

The Liberal Party sufficiently overcame its reservations not only to pre-select them both in later years, but to make each leader of the party, both in Opposition. Neither of these experiments was a happy one; Downer led the party for eight miserable months before resigning in January 1995 and Turnbull held out for thirteen before being whacked by his colleagues in late 2009.

"How do you like the job?" Downer asked Turnbull when he telephoned the prime minister from London in late 2015.

"It's absolutely brilliant! Best job ever. Fantastic! I'm absolutely loving it," Turnbull enthused.

Downer had a specific interest in Turnbull's response. In Adelaide for Christmas in 2013, just three months after Tony Abbott had been sworn in as

Australia's twenty-eighth prime minister, he had asked him the same question. The answer was very different.

"Oh," groaned Abbott, pulling a face. "It's such a hard job! It really is just so unbelievably difficult. Every morning I wake up and I can't believe it, how much of a responsibility it is."

Malcolm Turnbull and Tony Abbott have circled each other all their political lives, and have each been Opposition leader once and prime minister once. Each man has deprived the other of the Liberal leadership once, too. They both were journalists in their earlier lives. They have ridden out against each other – most notably, outside Canberra, in the republican debate. They have affected and confided in each other, and gone surfing together. They have said dreadful things to each other in moments of conflict, but have always found a way back to civility. Tony Abbott testifies that when he fell into a lengthy malaise after the Howard government's defeat, it was a spirited argument with Turnbull which spurred him to pull himself together.

And when Malcolm Turnbull called his new cabinet together after ending Tony Abbott's prime minister-ship before even its first term had elapsed, he told them: "I know what he's going through. I went through it myself, and it's the worst thing you can possibly go through. I was only Opposition leader when it hap-pened to me, so I can only imagine how much pain he's feeling. Anything that anyone can do to help him and ease his pain, please do."

But their experiences in office make a fascinating study in opposites. Tony Abbott relished his work as Opposition leader, a job into which he poured vast amounts of energy and enthusiasm. He was potent, focused, absolutely deadly, and ultimately he succeeded. The most abiding recollection of his Opposition leadership is the discipline with which he repeated his trio of slogans: *Stop the boats. Scrap the carbon tax. End the waste.*

So good was Tony Abbott, in fact, as Opposition leader, that he never entirely left the job. His most significant achievements as prime minister were acts of dismantlement or shutting down: ending the carbon and mining taxes, stopping the boats.

Malcolm Turnbull, in contrast, struggled as Opposition leader. He was often chippy and irritable. He grew quickly frustrated with colleagues and sometimes sought to overwhelm or bully them. He struggled, too, with the negative aspects of the job; if Abbott's biggest failure in government was that he used too much of his time as prime minister to take things apart, Turnbull's in opposition was that he overleapt his colleagues in an attempt to build something; his crowning misadventure was to seek a grand deal with the Labor Party on carbon pricing, a quasi-suicidal endeavour for which his party punished him with ultimate force.

It's an odd part of our political system that the traditional audition for the prime ministership is to be leader of the Opposition, when those two jobs have such different requirements. Bob Hawke, who served what he describes as "the ideal period" of one month as Opposition leader, says he wouldn't have been any good at the job longer term. "You've really got to love belting your opponents," he says. "That's the essence of it. It's just not my cup of tea. And you've got to have a capacity, I think, almost for hate to be a good Opposition leader, and I don't have that capacity at all."

Kim Beazley, Hawke offers, is an example of a Labor leader who would have been a better prime minister than he was an Opposition leader. "Kim was not a good Opposition leader because, if I can use the vernacular, he didn't have enough shit in him. If he'd won the '98 election, which he so nearly did, I think he would have made a great prime minister."

*

Some of the differences between Australia's twenty-eighth prime minister and its twenty-ninth are obvious. Malcolm Turnbull is more upbeat, more expansive ("waffly," his critics would say), less disciplined and less aggressive. Abbott freaked people out by eating onions and winking in radio interviews. Turnbull is more given to jovial digression. "I must say that I love this standing studio!" he enthused at the end of a fairly hostile exchange with Radio National breakfast host Fran Kelly. "Don't know if people watching us on television can see us standing ... It is so much better for us. We should all spend more time standing."

Unlike Abbott's, his staff appointments have been studiously uncontroversial. He cleaves closely to the decisions of his predecessor on contentious social issues. He has toned down the language on national security. Soon after coming to office, Turnbull discovered and scotched plans for significantly increased security at Parliament House, commissioned by Peta Credlin and Tony Abbott after the Lindt Café siege at Christmas 2014 and budgeted at $300 million. There were plans for a large structure to be built around the parliament's ministerial wing, creating a buffer around the prime minister's office, which currently occupies a section of the building's external wall, protected from the outside world by a courtyard and a steel gate. Other proposals included a large fence around the building, and then a concrete ditch around that, to exclude pedestrians. "This is a *moat*! It's ridiculous!" Turnbull protested when he learnt of the plans, and threw them out. Turnbull also reopened the corridors around the prime ministerial suite and removed the layers of builder's plastic which had been laid over the steel vehicular gates to the prime minister's courtyard, installed to obscure the line of sight from outside and assuage Credlin's fears that Tony Abbott would fall victim to sniper fire from a long-range rifleman or rocket-propelled grenade launcher.

Turnbull "stopped the moats," convinced that a political leader who chooses to live in a fortress thereby accepts a spirit of besiegement. He chafes at the $550,000 BMW commissioned by his predecessor, which features unpuncturable tyres and is designed to be invulnerable to AK-47 fire. It has only two seats in the back, and the prime minister – still mourning his dinky Prius – hates being unable to give more than one person a lift in his heavy new gas-guzzler. He continues to take the train wherever possible.

He likes to go kayaking on Sydney Harbour, while listening to podcasts. (One feels for the prime ministerial police detail. After six years of Rudd and Gillard, who lived obediently in the Lodge, fighting viciously among themselves but otherwise observing a decently sedentary lifestyle, suddenly there's Tony Abbott, who wants to live in barracks and cycle 80 kilometres before dawn, then Malcolm Turnbull, who favours his own waterfront home, small flimsy craft and public transport. His kayaking expeditions, apparently, are monitored closely by the water police, who chunter along in his wake as the twenty-ninth prime minister of Australia, happy as a clam, paddles across the harbour listening to Slate's *Political Gabfest*.)

The prime ministerial suite itself is perhaps the most-renovated patch of real estate in Parliament House. Six prime ministers it's hosted, in ten years. John Howard's green Chesterfields, the desk belonging to Menzies and the oil painting by Winston Churchill were trucked out in 2007 to be replaced by the burnt-orange tub chairs and Chinese artworks of Kevin Rudd. They were in turn usurped, three years later, by Julia Gillard's Sherrin football and Western Bulldogs scarf, whereafter the Churchill painting made a reappearance under Tony Abbott, along with the youthful portrait of Queen Elizabeth II that accompanies the Member for Warringah from office to office.

And in September 2015, the office underwent a Turnbull Rethink. Out went the Queen and Churchill. Up went the net value of office artworks, thanks to a large John Olsen painting commissioned by the Turnbulls – *Sydney Seaport Table* – which hangs nicely in the eye-line of any vigorous modern prime minister who happens to step up to the standing desk.

The modernity is no accident. Turnbull's genuine fascination for gadgetry is boundless. He was an early enthusiast for information technology, and made a bundle when he and his buddy Trevor Kennedy sold their stake in OzEmail in 1999 (Turnbull's cut was $57 million, from an initial investment of $500,000). He had a Kindle in parliament before they were even available for sale in Australia. His enthusiasm for the iPad, when it was invented, was that of a starving man for a sandwich. When the Apple Watch arrived, Turnbull had one straightaway.

The Fairfax photographer Alex Ellinghausen, in a wonderful 2015 article on photographing Australian political leaders, listed the individual tics that – over the years – became unmistakable photographic memes. Kevin Rudd's elaborate hair-flick. Julia Gillard's open-throated victory laugh, head thrown back, when she elicited a concession at the dispatch box. Bill Shorten's "Grumpy Cat" frown, in which the corners of his mouth turn comically down. Tony Abbott's wink (a tough one, this – harder to photograph than a snow leopard. "It's so quick that you have to pre-empt the shot when you feel it coming," explains Ellinghausen.)

So far, the two memes Malcolm Turnbull has given photographers are *Gesticulation with Spectacles* and *Checking the Apple Watch*.

Tony Abbott, who declared early in his leadership that he was no "tech head," never became one in prime ministerial office. He uses technology where necessary, with a Luddite tendency to stick to familiar ground. Years ago, when Abbott was a Howard government frontbencher writing regular newspaper columns, a staffer helped him with a computer problem and was horrified and amused to discover that the enthusiastic two-finger typist was using a single Word document to write all of his speeches and articles. He hadn't cottoned on to the fact that you could have more than one.

Turnbull's technological revolution, by comparison, is seemingly endless. In recent years, he has expanded boldly into discreet messaging platforms like Confide, Wickr and WhatsApp (favoured by political conspirators and sexters alike) for the capacity they offer of communications beyond even the considerable range of George Brandis's metadata recovery laws. Ministers flounder in his wake, crashing through the App Store in pursuit of whichever platform the man's currently using.

"I have always been very curious," is Turnbull's explanation. "So I've always enjoyed studying and reading and learning, and of course the fabulous thing about the internet is that all of the knowledge of the world is – you know – available on your smart-phone, so that's incredible." Regardless of Google's asymmetry of purpose with the federal tax system, Turnbull enthuses that "it's certainly done a great service to the curious."

Turnbull's delight in knowledge is – in the right moment – a powerfully charming attribute. In a political landscape increasingly choked by the smog of 24-hour opinion, sham outrage, grandstanding and the rest of the clutter that dogs a politician's day, a leader who still has the enthusiasm to look up the etymology of a crazy-sounding word *just for the fun of it* is a rare bird and a marvel to see.

Unsurprisingly, for a man constantly torn between real-life conversations and the siren call of the digital omniverse, Turnbull tends to switch on and off. You can be in an absorbing exchange with him and then notice that he has gone quiet, his conversational contribution reduced to the occasional sonorous "Mmmmm." Then you realise that he's fidgeting away at his phone, or is subtly vetting phone messages.

Waiting with him in an airline lounge once, I plumped down in a seat next to him and asked if he wanted a cup of tea; I was fetching one for myself. Knitting his eyebrows and staring straight ahead, he replied sternly: "Well, I can't see how *that* could possibly work." Scanning his face for clues (perhaps he was a coffee man?), I noticed the flash of the busy

Bluetooth device clipped to his ear, realised my error and stole away.

Sometimes, he can be in two places at once. In April 2010 the Walkley Foundation arranged a panel discussion on media and politics, featuring Turnbull, recently dethroned as Opposition leader, Laurie Oakes, the ABC journalist Quentin Dempster and the US journalist and academic John Nichols. I was on the panel too; it was too big a group for the purposes of the discussion, and by about the fifteen-minute mark Malcolm had pulled out his iPad and his smart-phone and was scanning both. Fascinated, and sitting immediately to his left, I peered out of the corner of my eye at what he was doing. Emails on the phone, as far as I could make out. On the iPad, an article with diagrams that looked a bit aqueducty.

Five minutes later, the panel discussion arrived at the gristly heart of the media-and-politics argument: are politicians naturally just shallow and cowardly, or are they trained to be that way? Oakes quoted Tony Abbott's recent comment that he "wasn't looking at any policies that went further than his lifetime." It was, said Oakes glumly, not a very inspiring attitude.

Suddenly, Turnbull surfaced from the world of Appian plumbing and push notifications. Removing his glasses and waving them (that gesture!) with a calorific smile, he interjected: "But then, Laurie, you do have to remember: he *is* incredibly fit."

The periods of inattention don't always end with a game-saving one-liner. For all Malcolm Turnbull's lifelong career as a deal-maker, he has a terrible poker face. Just as it's easy to see when he is seized and intrigued by an issue or a conversation or a person, it's easy to see when he isn't. It's like a little light going off. When he's bored by a conversation, his eyes wander. His fingers creep towards his smart-phone. He wants to get back to the universe, with all its thrilling possibility.

When he's in a press conference that bores him, his sentences get rangy and circuitous, like the tracks of a lost dog. He'll trail off, start a new one. Sometimes it looks compellingly as though he is trying to jog his own interest. On bad days, it looks aimless.

On one level, it's perfectly understandable that Malcolm Turnbull would have quite a low boredom threshold. To a man who has fought hand-to-hand with Kerry Packer and survived, gone searching for gold in Siberia and teamed up with a reviled former spy to win a towering, unlikely victory over the government of Margaret Thatcher, it's easy to see how the duller encounters of government – the board-room lunches with their ranks of suits, the endless fundraisers with their mutually obsequious small talk or interactions with busybodies who just want to tell you *this one thing* – might seem rather thin gruel. There are wild cards which always pique his interest: a pert child, an entrepreneur doing something wildly innovative, someone who knows a lot about water.

There is no doubt of Turnbull's charm. "He's one of the most charming people I've ever met," says a cabinet colleague. "He can deploy his charm like a lethal weapon." But there is charm, and then there is political charm. Political charm is being able to summon the ordinary kind at a moment's notice. Even when you are tired, even when you couldn't think of anything on earth about which you could possibly care less than this conversation, even when the half-finished article in the *Economist* is calling you so strongly that you can almost read it like Braille on the phone in your pocket. Political charm is no one being able to tell when you're bored. Malcolm Turnbull is working on that, but he's not there yet.

One business observer says that while Turnbull's government is an improvement on Abbott's in that ministers genuinely have carriage of issues and Turn-bull himself is accessible, there is no mistaking the junctures at which he is tired or unfocused. "The face that says 'Gosh, I'd rather not be here,' is so evident," he laughs. "You never got that with John Howard, who was so professional, you never knew when he was tired, he always looked and sounded exactly the same – interested, courteous, engaged."

"I think at his best he can be extraordinary," says a colleague. "Malcolm is a real confidence player. You can tell when he's across something, he believes in it and he knows why he's doing it. The challenge is: how do you get him to feel that way more often?"

The universe is never far from Turnbull's fingers. Even in meetings he's chairing as prime minister, when there's a dispute underway, Turnbull is quick to call in Apple's third umpire. Not as much as he used to do, but it's still there.

"He still has to be the smartest person in the room – he can't help that," says one minister. "You'll be having a talk with him and he'll pull out his iPad and look up some legal precedent or whatever, just to settle the argument. It's endearing, because you have someone who's quite genuinely learned running the show, but it's annoying because you're all sitting in this meeting and he's burrowing into 1920s constitutional law."

Turnbull's ambition is boundless. He came to the job of prime minister determined to change not only the government and the way it did business, but the nature of politics itself. He resisted advice from colleagues to go to an election soon after he became prime minister, because he did not wish to be seen as a cheap political opportunist. He opted instead – in the end – for the longest election campaign in memory despite every historical precedent shrieking that long campaigns are very bad news, especially for leaders who have not fought any campaigns at all before. He wanted to end the bitterness and negativity of Australian politics, and tackle personally the accelerated news cycle by making decisions in a slow and deliberative way, not driven by ideology or expediency or panic in the face of the daily media churn.

All these decisions violated, in their own way, certain rules of politics. Never have a long campaign. Always go to an election when you're best placed to win it. Feed the media beast, or it will feed on you. But Malcolm Turnbull, in all his years, has never been one to obey convention. In business and in law, his most distinctive feature was his capacity for deep insurrection to the orthodoxies of his environment. His faith – very often justified, it must be said – was that brilliance and force could overcome such barriers.

And when he became prime minister he intended, by sheer force of personality, to transform a political culture that has broken five prime ministers in a decade. He's always aimed high.

Don't Be Dull

Australia has for ten years now been in a death roll of leadership instability. The long-held rhythm of Australian politics (elect a government in the House of Representatives, devise a Senate that will make that government's life a merry hell, then wait usually a term or so too long before giving someone else a go) has given way to a hiccupy succession of new prime ministers who barely survive their probation periods. Six prime ministers in ten years: John Howard, then Kevin Rudd, then Julia Gillard, then Rudd again, then Tony Abbott, and now Malcolm Turnbull.

The only decade in Australian history to record a higher rate of prime ministerial job-swapping than 2006–16 was the very first decade of Australia's life as a nation, after federation in 1901. Over those ten years, Australia swore in eight prime ministers, some of them multiple times: from the auspicious and slightly bungled appointment of Edmund Barton in 1901, we went to Alfred Deakin in 1903, to Chris

Watson the year after that, then to George Reid in 1905, then back to Deakin, then Andrew Fisher, then Deakin *again*, then Fisher again.

For ten years now, Australian voters have been unable to do what we like to do with prime ministers, which is forget them entirely while we go about our business, content that someone is steering the ship in a manner vaguely predictable to us. For these ten years, we've been unable to look away, as new prime minister after new prime minister arrives in office, full of promises and plans to tear down the work of their immediate predecessor and build something ambitious in its stead.

And so, in that time, we have greeted emissions trading schemes and water schemes and broadband schemes and car industry packages and medical research schemes and national disability insurance schemes and new industrial regimes and new levies and Defence white papers – and sometimes we have said goodbye to them again within a year when the next PM turns up.

This time, the next PM is – on the basis of his pedigree alone – the most exciting man in Australian politics. He is personally quite excited about the upturn in his fortunes, and would like the excitement to be shared. "There has never been a more exciting time to be alive than today and there has never been a more exciting time to be an Australian!" he declared, in his first public statement after his party decided to make him prime minister.

His MPs have adopted "There's never been a more exciting time" as a little joke for every time they do something in their electorates. There's never been a more exciting time to open a treatment works! There's never been a more exciting time to encourage small businesses to utilise the government's instant asset write-off! It is a format that lends itself easily to the kind of black humour in which election-year MPs are so quick to indulge. "There's never been a more exciting time to find out from the newspaper that your leader is redrawing federation!" texted one in late March.

So personally entwined is Malcolm Turnbull with the concept of increased animation, in fact, that when the publicly funded advertising campaign for the government's innovation package went to air using the term "exciting time," Labor complained to the auditor-general that it was a free political plug for the prime minister.

It may be the first time that the auditor-general has been asked to adjudicate on degrees of excitement. It is possibly an unfair request.

But the awkward thing for Malcolm Turnbull – a lifelong omnithusiast and irrepressible change agent – is that not everyone wants excitement. Very particularly, his own colleagues in the Coalition party room remember some very bad things about Malcolm Turnbull's personal brand of excitement (trying to chivvy them into an audacious deal with Labor on climate change, the mesmerising strategic overshoot that was the Godwin Grech affair) and would prefer things to be quieter. All leaders have at least two constituencies: their immediate colleagues, whom they have to keep on side, and their broader electorates, whom they have to win over.

And the clearest possible conclusion from Malcolm Turnbull's first six months in office is that his dominant priority has been the first-mentioned group. From his first hours as leader, in which he agreed to a set of demands from the National Party (handing over responsibility for water to the junior Coalition partner, agreeing to a serious retwiddling of the competition laws to crimp the market power of supermarket giants), Turnbull has striven to keep a peaceable party room. The eye-catching causes to which he has attached himself over the years – the republic, same-sex marriage, emissions trading – have been muted by Prime Minister Turnbull. On the republic, he says the time is not now. On same-sex marriage, he is maintaining the plans for a plebiscite laid by Tony Abbott, despite having opposed the idea initially. He is no longer pushing for the emissions trading scheme that cost him the Liberal leadership the first time around. More than that: he is actively campaigning against Labor in its 2016 policy to impose, again, a price on carbon emissions.

Prime Minister Turnbull's biggest reforms in office have been determinedly fine-print affairs. Media ownership laws, the installation – as requested by the National Party – of an effects test in section 46 of the *Competition and Consumer Act*. Even Senate reform – easily the most significant of Turnbull's achievements, and the subject of his most swashbuckling political manoeuvre so far – is rather bland chaff for those who have habitually associated Malcolm Bligh Turnbull with an elevated pulse rate.

"Don't be dull!" I remember Turnbull telling journalists at his first and only Christmas drinks hosted as Opposition leader, back in 2008. Seven years later, we're at the strangest of crossroads; we're an exciting country at an exciting time, led by an exciting man whose first task – in the office he's dreamed about all his exciting life – is to be as dull as possible.

*

Turnbull has wasted very little of his life being dull, and his life before politics has done several things for him. First, it's made him very rich. Second, it's made

him some enemies. Third, it's given him an inex-
haustible supply of dinner-party anecdotes.

Silvery threads connect him – through his family,
and through his deeds – to all manner of people. "Six
Degrees of Malcolm Turnbull," in which any famous
person in the world can be connected to Turnbull
within six steps, would be a feasible party game. John
F. Kennedy? Okay: from Kennedy we make an easy
leap to his showbiz friend Frank Sinatra, and thence
to Sinatra's fellow rat-packer Humphrey Bogart.
Who starred in *Casablanca* with Ingrid Bergman,
who was leading lady in *Gaslight*, which was also the
screen debut in 1944 for a very young Angela Lansbury, whose cousin Coral ten years later gave birth to
her first and only child, Malcolm Turnbull.

Mick Jagger? That's even easier. Jagger is a one-
time guest of Brixton Prison, having been briefly
incarcerated there in 1967 after police busted him with
a modest quantity of illicit mood-enhancement pills.
Another former Brixton prisoner is Malcolm Turnbull's great-great-uncle, the former British Labour
leader George Lansbury. Lansbury, as Labour mayor
of Poplar in 1921, did six weeks in Brixton as a pen-
alty for redistributing council tax income to the needy
rather than funnelling it to London; this heroic gesture produced the term "Poplarism" and transformed
Lansbury into a folk hero.

Lansbury emigrated briefly to Australia in 1884 with his wife and three children, but was so horrified by the harsh conditions that he herded his family back to Britain and commenced a political campaign against the British authorities for distributing misleading propaganda to potential emigrants.

Lansbury's staunch pacifism (he remains the only major-party leader in the UK to have responded to the threat of war by calling for immediate, full disarmament) cost him dearly within the Labour Party and he eventually stood down as leader in 1935. The socialist writer Beatrice Webb, evaluating Lansbury's life and work, was driven regretfully to the conclusion that while he was a "great heart," he suffered from being an "emotional non-thinker." As so often happens in politics, the times did not suit him.

Malcolm Turnbull's life is full of recurrent themes, little refrains or trails of coincidence that add an extra sparkle to his unlikely biography.

His grandfather, Oscar Lansbury, was the head of sound effects at the ABC, devising gunshots and the clip-clopping of horses' feet for radio plays, seventy-five years before his daughter's only son would assume responsibility for the broadcaster as communications minister in the Abbott government. Oscar, an opera singer, had come out from England – along with Turnbull's grandmother, May – as part of the touring cast of *Showboat*. "*Showboat* regrettably ran aground in Melbourne during the Depression you see," Turnbull explains. "The producers unfortunately ran out of money and couldn't pay for the fare home, and so that's how they ended up in Australia."

Coral – Oscar's daughter – was a prolific young radio playwright, who at twenty-four married her godfather, a man forty years her senior. He died within the year of liver disease, whereupon she married Bruce Turnbull, and gave birth to her only son, Malcolm.

At times, the Turnbull life-story seems almost to have the silvery impermanence of cinema, and you suspect that somewhere behind it all is a haggard old-time Hollywood screenwriter, artfully inserting plot twists and complex little synchronicities for the benefit of the audience. The screenwriter has relied, for the fundamentals, on a classic rags-to-riches theme.

Smart boy, not much dough, abandoned by his mother at eight, left alone a lot as a kid, sent to boarding school, loving but absent father, forced to rely on own brilliance. Busy university life, period of brisk womanising, moonlights as brilliant young journalist, snapped up by grumpy tycoon. Rhodes Scholar, famed barrister, fabulous clever wife, adorable family, filthy-rich banker, substantial philanthropist, stormed into parliament, breezed into cabinet, seized the Liberal leadership, lost it in a horrid fight with his own party, decided to quit parliament, changed his mind, became a cabinet minister again, then – twelve years into his formal political career – found his happy ending.

Don't think that this is a mere fairy story, either; our scriptwriter has clearly worked with Orson Welles, for there's plenty of darkness too. Our hero is flawed: he can be impatient and mercurial, and his life is littered with people who cannot forgive him his victories, feeling them ill-gotten. It's as though he has a poisoned sword. The wounds he has inflicted on others don't seem to go away; they tend to canker and are nursed bitterly by the injured, sometimes for years and years.

Often this is a phenomenon exacerbated by his own ability to move on blithely from conflict. It's as if this lifelong business of getting somewhere bears him swiftly away from such human wreckage; personally he does not hold grudges for long, and often seems mildly surprised – even, in some cases, a bit indignant – when someone he maimed in court or business years ago still has a hard word for him.

What is it that has powered this restless, tireless drive through life, apart from talent?

Lucille Iremonger, whose study of British prime ministers between 1809 and 1937 was called *The Fiery*

Chariot, found that of twenty-four leaders in that period, fifteen had lost a parent in childhood.

Malcolm Gladwell, in *David and Goliath*, points out that twelve American presidents lost their fathers in childhood; he coins the term "eminent orphans" to describe the ranks of successful men and women in business and science who are the survivors of child-hood heartbreak and loss.

It's a pattern that runs noticeably through Aus-tralian politics; there's Kevin Rudd, Paul Keating and Mark Latham, who lost fathers young; Bob Hawke, who lost a brother in whose shadow he had lived. And Malcolm Turnbull, whose need to achieve, to be successful, to show his mother what he could do, is a casebook study for Iremonger.

"If I look back, you know, perhaps I was thinking to myself, you know, if, even if unconsciously: if I work harder and do better, will she come back?" Turnbull himself reflected in an *Australian Story* interview in 2009. "I guess prime minister probably would have been good enough for her, but ... [*laughs*] but maybe it wouldn't have been good enough."

Sent to boarding school in Sydney at the age of eight when his parents' marriage began to fail, the young Malcolm had a miserable time of it. Desperately lonely and sometimes bullied, he nevertheless felt terrified of disappointing his absent parents. On one occasion, when a school report ranked him at about the middle of the top-stream class of boys rather than right at the top, he was too afraid to send it to his mother.

Lucy Turnbull recalls that the extraordinary expectations of Malcolm – and his determination to fulfil them, rather than rebel – were both very obvious to her and very striking when she first met him.

"Both parents put incredible pressure on him to succeed," she says. "It was very intense. It was the most remarkable thing. I thought it was amazing that this person wasn't actually a heroin addict or something."

"Look, Coral was a fantastic mother ... till she left!" Turnbull told me, laughing, in 2013. "She was brilliant! But she just, I think, I don't know ... I suspect that she sort of got bored with the role."

One hesitates to be too glib about these things, but it is hard not to spot – in the life of Malcolm Turnbull, with its natural bent towards grand ambition, overachievement and high drama – the bone-deep need of a small boy to recapture that attention, to make that role into something for which a thrill-seeking mother might be motivated to return.

Bruce never spoke ill of Coral to her son. Did this teach him something about not holding grudges, I asked him.

"I've just seen, over the years, so many people crippled by hatred," Turnbull replied. "And I just think that hatred corrodes the hater. It does more damage to the hater than it can ever conceivably do to the person that you're hating and so you're just better off getting all of those negative emotions out of your life."

Lucy Turnbull says her husband is "not a festerer." "The compassion and unconditional love that he had for his mother is what won out, despite the enormous grief that had really marked his emotional life for some time."

The abandonment by his mother produced – rather than rancour – a determination in Turnbull that his life, and the lives of his children, would be different. When Malcolm and Lucy married – young – both swore that their marriage would not fall apart as each of their parents' marriages had. To this day, they are an extraordinarily tight couple. They are endlessly in touch, texting or telephoning. When they are in the same room, they cross-reference stories and memories, things they've read, art they've seen. Sometimes, they read the same book at the same time, their two bookmarks chasing each other through the pages. They have been business partners, charitable collaborators and legal colleagues, as well as parents to Alex and Daisy and grandparents to Daisy's son, Jack. They have counselled each other through terrible political difficulties: his loss of the Liberal leadership in 2009, her sacking as lord mayor of Sydney in 2004 by the NSW government led by Bob Carr, once one of the couple's closest friends.

Malcolm Turnbull's mother left a vacuum in his life, and he has filled it in part with swaggering deeds, but to a far greater extent, he has filled it with Lucy Hughes.

"One of the absolute keys to Malcolm is his unhappy childhood," says one colleague. "The other is the spectacular success of his marriage. It's one of the happiest marriages that I've observed in my life. There's nothing phony about it. They are best friends and a mutual admiration society and a thorough support to each other."

*

It was George Lansbury's outrage at the injustice of life in Australia that drove him into politics a century ago. His great-great-nephew took a more circuitous, if more spectacular, path. Unlike most practitioners, Malcolm Turnbull was not made famous by politics. He was famous already, having reaped abundant headlines as Kerry Packer's Boy Friday, as the cheeky advocate of the *Spycatcher* case, and as the captain of the doomed ship HMAS *Australian Republic*.

Turnbull was not, like some of his colleagues, driven to enter politics because of some galvanising injustice that nagged and fretted at him. He did not storm into politics to strike a blow for small business against Paul

Keating, as – for instance – many new Liberal MPs did in 1996. Quite the reverse; the mid-1990s found Malcolm Turnbull discussing, with various Labor figures including Keating, the prospect of his recruitment as a Labor parliamentarian. "Initiated by Keating!" protests Turnbull, who says he refused the approach. "Initiated by Turnbull!" insists Graham Richardson, who wrote that Turnbull petitioned him in 1993 for a Senate spot but legged it on being told about the tender delights of grassroots ALP membership.

So what is he doing in politics? This is a question that has occupied colleagues and staffers in countless happy hours of speculation since his arrival in Canberra in 2004. Unlike John Howard, Malcolm Turnbull was not driven by an ideological program of specific reforms; the teenage Turnbull, one imagines, went to bed dreaming of one day becoming prime minister, while Howard's night-time reveries were complicated affairs in which he single-handedly dismantled Australia's system of centralised wage-fixing.

Turnbull was driven into politics partly by aptitude and ambition, partly by a sense of public service and partly, one suspects, by the gravitational pull of fate. "A force of nature" is how Tim Costello once described him, and this is a variation on an oft-repeated theme among colleagues, many of whom, from the moment of his nomination for the seat of Wentworth, viewed Turnbull as a sort of galloping inevitability – something to be *got through*, like puberty or chickenpox.

In the broad church that is the Liberal Party, there is room for all sorts of approaches. But Malcolm Turnbull is frighteningly breezy about some things that really set the pearls rattling in the pews. His blithe acceptance that sometimes gambits will fail, for instance, is a sine qua non among venture capitalists, but very exotic indeed among modern politicians, who feel very deeply the widespread expectation that they should be infallible. And he doesn't have the instinctive horror of higher taxes that is – for many Liberals – a chromosomal feature. He has had close personal friendships with three former Labor premiers. He was in business with Neville Wran.

To the Liberal Party of John Howard, Malcolm Turnbull for a long time was like a handsome stranger who turns up on a cruise boat: charming, witty, erudite and happy to buy the drinks. So why, oh why, hang back?

It can't be a "new money" thing. The Liberal Party does not have the same sensitivity to this as does the British Conservative Party, where it was once disparagingly said of Margaret Thatcher's challenger Michael Heseltine that he "bought his own furniture."

It's more a "new membership" thing. The Liberal Party is like a gentlemen's club, in some respects. Anyone can join, and be treated politely. But after a few years, when you notice you're not getting anywhere, it might occur to you that in some way you are not quite the ticket. To some in the Liberal Party, the Malcolm Turnbull who arrived in parliament in 2004 was not quite the ticket.

"Malcolm doesn't always realise that in the Liberal Party, when somebody raises an eyebrow at you, it actually means something," laughs one Liberal warhorse, a supporter of Turnbull.

As a result, Turnbull has committed howlers. Like the time he was addressing his colleagues and pointed out to them the curious habit Kevin Rudd had of mentioning him – Turnbull – all the time. "Neville Wran, whom I regard as a great political strategist, told me he made it a practice never to mention his opponents by name," Turnbull informed the meeting. Or the time – again at a party meeting – when he mused aloud on his suspicion that the former Labor prime minister Paul Keating was coaching Rudd and Swan behind the scenes. "I rang Keating, and I said to him: 'You're helping them, aren't you?'" Turnbull told his flock.

Now, in front of any other crowd, neither of these remarks would seem exceptional, let alone exceptionable. But Liberal MPs are a sensitive lot, and the effect was rather like a meeting of Orangemen hearing their preacher make a breezy reference to having phoned the Pope the other day.

As it happens, Keating *was* helping Rudd: with free assessments of Turnbull. As the *Sydney Morning Herald*'s Peter Hartcher reported in 2009:

> When Malcolm Turnbull took the leadership of the Liberal Party, Paul Keating ... told the incumbent Labor Prime Minister on the phone that he had studied Turnbull over the years. Rudd had to understand three key things about Turnbull. First, he should know that Turnbull was brilliant. Second, that Turnbull was utterly fearless. At this point Rudd, an irritated Rudd, demanded to know, "Is there any good news here?" Keating replied with his third point: Turnbull has no judgment.

It's the instincts of Malcolm Turnbull that gave some Liberals a heart attack; his ignorance of or lack of fealty to the party's unwritten social or cultural codes. When Turnbull – then shadow treasurer – was asked in May 2008 about the controversy surrounding the new photographic works of Bill Henson, for example, he gave an instinctively libertarian reply: "I think we have ... a culture of great artistic freedom in this country and I don't believe the vice squad's role is to go into art galleries." Turnbull was the only politician in Australia who voiced any support for Henson during the national outbreak of moralistic fervour that accompanied that artist's fateful exhibition, which was staged at the Roslyn Oxley9 Gallery, in Turnbull's electorate.

Labor prime minister Kevin Rudd led the charge, calling Henson's images of adolescents "revolting." (It was an extreme call. Particularly given Rudd's private admiration for the work of the late Donald Friend – an actual and self-confessed pederast – several of whose paintings used to hang in the private sitting-room of the Rudd prime ministerial office.)

Turnbull's comments whizzed around the parliamentary Liberal Party, many of whose members felt that his response demonstrated a chronic lack of judgment. All very well to support artists, it was felt, but not in public – not when sentiment against Henson's work was running so high. The then leader of the party, Brendan Nelson, declared, on behalf of the Liberals, that Henson's images of naked children "violated Australian values." After he made those remarks, Nelson received a call from Malcolm Turnbull, always on the front foot. Turnbull berated him: "Do you know how many art galleries I have in my electorate?"

The journalist David Penberthy, writing on the now-defunct News Limited website *The Punch*, reported a gentle attempt by Howard himself to remonstrate with his art-loving leadership successor. Meeting Turnbull at the 2008 NRL grand final, Penberthy records, Howard playfully grabbed Turnbull's shoulders and turned him towards the general admission stands, saying, "Look over there, Malcolm. Ninety-five per cent of those people think Bill Henson is a pervert."

Howard was trying to assist Turnbull; he knew as well as anyone how lumpy a fit Malcolm Turnbull was with the contemporary party he created. The wider population looks at Turnbull with interest, curious to see what he will turn out to be like. But his party is full of people who look to his past, and fear they already know.

Experiments in Hyperactivity: The Early Years

Not all Liberal MPs went to university. In fact, over the course of the Howard era it became a distinct advantage not to have been to university. But those Liberal MPs who edged into student politics and thence found themselves swept into the powerful currents of grown-up politics tended to have very different university lives from the one lived by Malcolm Turnbull.

Here's John Howard, for instance, speaking about his years of higher study: "I was fairly non-involved at the university. I just did my course. When I was at university, I had a lot of trouble with my hearing. I wore a hearing aid for about eighteen months and I think that had a slightly inhibiting effect ... I tended just to be involved in study and in playing sport at the weekend."

Turnbull, by contrast, found so much time for extracurricular activities that he seemed often at grave risk of abandoning the academic experiment altogether. While studying arts and law at the University of Sydney from 1973, Turnbull worked freelance for,

as he put it, "a leftish weekly called *Nation Review*."
By 1976 he had managed to install himself in the
NSW parliamentary press gallery and, while playing
hooky from his university studies, filed reports for
Nation Review, for the Catholic Church–owned
radio station 2SM, and for Kerry Packer's Channel
Nine. As he put it: "I was serving, simultaneously,
Marx, God and Mammon."

Turnbull supplemented these income streams by
flogging jingles to John Singleton, the adman who in
1977 introduced the young Turnbull to Kerry Francis Bullmore Packer. Already something of an
entrepreneur, Turnbull dealt with the consequent
traffic jam of demands on his time by outsourcing
what he could.

At the reasonable rate of thirty dollars a week plus
expenses, he hired a friend, John O'Sullivan, to attend
lectures and take notes for him.

The mid-'70s were turbulent years on campuses
around Australia. As Turnbull began his university
career, Liberal students busied themselves with out-
rages against the Whitlam government or fought
Trotskyists in the unique cublike rough-and-tumble
that constitutes university politics. When Whitlam
was dismissed, a sizeable protest was staged against
the governor-general, Sir John Kerr, at the University
of New South Wales. Tony Abbott, an irreverent

young conservative from the University of Sydney, promptly organised a pro-Kerr rally.

In Melbourne, a young Peter Costello and his friend Michael Kroger were caught up in a melee when the new prime minister, Malcolm Fraser, visited Monash University in 1975. Later, Costello was thumped by a campus Trotskyist in a crucial rite of passage. Eighteen days before the Whitlam government was dismissed in 1975, Turnbull celebrated a milestone birthday. "In response to popular demand, Malcolm Turnbull is turning twenty-one," the party invitations read.

Turnbull seemed to be on a different course from that travelled by the average young Liberal pup. He developed a fascination with the ancient, poisonous and anti-Semitic figure of Jack Lang, the former Labor premier of New South Wales. During his first year at university, Turnbull regularly took a tape recorder and toiled up to the little Nithsdale Street office where Lang published his newspaper, the *Century*, until well into his tenth decade.

Turnbull, with his unreliable tape recorder, was there not just to soak up Lang's peppery epithets. Bizarrely enough, he was planning to write a musical about Lang, in collaboration with the late Bob Ellis.

"I was already a well-known writer by then," said Ellis of their meeting in about 1973. "I had a girl-friend who I lost, and she turned up again with

Malcolm about eighteen months after she left me, and to my chagrin I got to like him. He seemed roughly like he does now, which is a kind of somewhat naive and likeable and driven but essentially shy sort of fellow. We then used to go out rooting, and we would find ourselves alternatively in the same beds with different women and so on."

The musical was to have been called *Lang Is Right!*. The project itself – perhaps unsurprisingly – collapsed, and never made it to the stage.

"The whole purpose of all the taping was to write this damn thing, but I was of course egocentric and always doing other things," Ellis told me years ago. "Eventually [Turnbull] came around to discuss the play and I didn't want to see him, and so told him to fuck off. He broke the door down and raged at us till dawn, which intervention caused us to move to the northern beaches."

The tapes of Turnbull and Lang's conversations survive, somewhere inside Malcolm and Lucy Turnbull's house. Of the musical, not much remains. When I asked him about it, Turnbull said at first that he might still have it. A couple of weeks later, he sent an email to pronounce it lost. But Ellis claimed he still had a scrap or two, and showed me one scene in which Adolf Hitler appears before a group of "fat capitalists." Hitler comes across as trenchant, with a hint of camp (although in fairness this might just be the format).

> You who are men of high and lofty station
> Of noble birth and high school education
> With families full of generals, kings and princes
> I could hardly expect you to know where Linz is.

He is seeking liquidity:

> Tonight I will not ask for much; just a short solici-
> tation;
> Ten million marks, your blessing, and your kind
> co-operation …
> My way of doing business may not appeal to you;
> But tread softly lest you find yourself included
> with the Jew.

The refrain imparts an almost danceable feel:

> Just a little one step, two step, three step,
> Just a little goose step, four;
> Just a little bit of "Heil, Mein Führer"
> Just a little bit of war.

When I read these snippets to Turnbull, he laughed and insisted that they were not part of the musical.

"God, no. Hitler did not make an appearance. Bob must be mixed up," he said. "I do remember that there was this dreadful line, set in McNamara's Bookshop where Lang met his wife, that rhymed 'Patagonia' with 'new Australian utopia.' It was terrible."

The Hitler verses are in Turnbull's handwriting; they match another memento in Ellis's collection, a little poem titled "A Song, by Malcolm Turnbull." Are they part of the Lang musical? Ellis thought so. But Ellis has been wrong before, and Turnbull says he doesn't remember them at all.

"I remember at one point there was this marvellous exchange," said Ellis, who listened to some of the tapes of the teenager and the old man, "where you can hear Lang saying sharply, 'What do you mean? What do you mean it's not going?' And Malcolm, who's fiddling with the tape, says, 'I think it's all right.' And Lang barks: 'My time's valuable!'"

A digression here is warranted to note that *Lang is Right!* was by no means Turnbull's only stab at the poetry game. He won, in 1974, the University of Sydney poetry prize named for Henry Lawson, who happened to be Jack Lang's brother-in-law.

Turnbull's winning entry was a dreadful piece of doggerel entitled "A Woman is Just a Woman, But a Good Cigar is a Smoke." Turnbull wrote the poem as a speech for a debate on the topic of the title and

garnered such an uproarious reception that he sub-
mitted it for the Lawson Prize and won.

The poem spins the yarn of an outback pub called
the Golden Bandicoot, whose publican, Sam McPhee,
discovers that when the drovers come in from months
of isolation, it is not the company of the fairer sex
that they crave, but the hot blast of a fine cigar.

> So he spurred up his horse and rode like the wind
> for the "Golden Bandicoot"
> And hoped that he'd soon be wrapping his lips
> round a smouldering fat cheroot.
> He leapt off his horse and burst like a shell
> through the hotel's swinging door,
> Fixed Sam McPhee with a madman's gaze, "you
> know what I've come here for."

Looking back, Turnbull remembers his mother
being horrified that he should win the Henry Lawson
Prize with such a romp. Coral had won it herself back
in the 1940s, she told him, for a far more worthy work.

Back to Lang. Turnbull was by no means the only
nascent political leader who crept up the steps to
Lang's lair. Paul Keating was a teenage haunter of the
Century office ten years before Turnbull, and in 1971
campaigned successfully to have Lang, then ninety-
five, readmitted to the Labor Party.

Mark Latham, federal Labor's short-lived leader of 2003 and 2004, also found much to admire in Lang, and published an article on him in 1992 with the collaboration of Lang's son, Chris.

"For all his firebrand ways and capacity of stirring trouble within the ALP, Lang merely used the tools available to him to maximum effect as a politician," wrote Latham, in whose violent political tactics more than a sniff of Langishness was evident. "In public life it was ever thus."

"What it was that drew them to the rancorous old mountebank, then in his nineties, and his endless festering defamations of the dead, may lie in their similar souls and in their similar teenage dreams of rapid glory," wrote Ellis in a piece for the ABC website *Unleashed*, in late 2008. "In Lang's bellowing monomania, his rancid certitude, his boofheaded political martyrdom, his Catholic nepotistic tribalism, his messianic, hectoring style they found, I guess, as young men do, a pleasing role model, a Labor legend to follow like a pillar of fire through the wilderness of this world to, yes, a political martyrdom of their own."

Turnbull, for his part, has had a lifetime fascination for difficult political figures. He travelled to Britain while at university and interviewed Enoch Powell, the former Conservative MP and fiery orator who was sacked from the party's front bench in 1968 after his infamous "Rivers of Blood" speech about race relations. Continuing to America on the same trip, he tried to interview the disgraced Richard Nixon but had no luck.

Turnbull, who wrote an obituary of Lang in 1975 for the *Nation Review*, seemed drawn to Lang's "whatever it takes" approach.

The grandest of Lang's suicidal gestures, of course, and the trigger for his eventual dismissal, is found in the great dispute of the early 1930s over his repudiation of New South Wales's crippling interest payments to Britain. In order to evade court orders from the Commonwealth, Lang instructed his public servants to collect the state's revenues in cash. He barricaded the state treasury and set unemployed timber workers to guard it, vowing to spend his state's money on the poor of New South Wales, not the wealthy of London.

Lang went down, but there is a throb of heroism in his tactics that yet causes certain hearts to beat faster. The fact that Lang's tactics so closely mirrored those of Malcolm Turnbull's own maternal great-great-uncle (handing out taxes as alms comes straight from the Poplarist playbook) might explain some of Malcolm Turnbull's interest.

"If Lang's depression politics appear wild and misguided, it is only because of the comparison with the 'safe' and inhumanly cautious policies of the other governments of the day," argued the young Turnbull in his obituary for the *Nation Review*. "Like Roosevelt, Oswald Mosley and even Hitler, Lang was advocating, ahead of his time, reflationist solutions to the depression."

Thin ice, this. And very much indicative of the old man's force of personality. A few afternoons in Lang's company and you're already thinking, well, Hitler may have been a bastard, but he had some good economic policies.

The thrill of being a visionary, though, of perishing in the pursuit of a bold cause, condemned for being ahead of one's time – is it so very hard to identify, in the 21-year-old obituarist, the seeds of the Liberal leader who would in 2009 declare himself unable to lead a party that did not share his own belief in the urgency of addressing climate change?

The grown-up Turnbull is – to be fair – in many respects far more cautious about Lang. "He was a very colourful personality and he was larger than life in every respect," he ventured, in defence of his early interest. "He was also alive – apart from Bill McKell, there were no other politicians from the 1920s who were still around. He was filled with vituperation and venom. I wouldn't ever have wanted to have one zillionth of his bitterness.

"As my understanding of that period developed, and I talked to McKell, I really accepted his view eventually that Lang was a bit of a coward."

*

We cannot conclude any discussion of Turnbull's early years without visiting an incident which has trailed him unshakeably all the way through his eventful life. To friend and foe alike, the story is known simply as "The Cat."

"The Cat" has many functions. In the hands of some narrators, it's allegory. In others, it's pure fable. There are people who will swear blind that it is fact. And it serves as a rough indicator of general opinion on Turnbull.

So what are the facts, in the case of The People v Malcolm Turnbull (ex parte The Cat)? Turnbull, in about 1977 – before he met Lucy – knocked around with a young woman by the name of Fiona Watson, who lived in a tiny single-storey terrace in Double Bay. She was a remarkably beautiful young woman, and the young Turnbull was besotted with her. To complicate matters, or possibly to enhance them, she was the stepdaughter of the Labor senator and wit "Diamond" Jim McClelland.

By all accounts it was a turbulent relationship, and for reasons that are now lost to us, Miss Watson decided to end it; she had no shortage of suitors. Turnbull, who even then was not one to accept defeat lightly, embarked upon a passionate letter-writing campaign directed at Miss Watson's cat, an animal of which she was inordinately fond. In the letters, Turnbull exhorts the beast to intercede with its mistress and convince her to take him back. As a romantic technique, it errs towards the Elizabethan. But who are we, after all these years, to question the epistolary methods of a young man who has lost his girl? The real intrigue set in later, when Miss Watson arrived home one day to find the cat, dead, outside her house.

No evidence exists to connect Malcolm Turnbull with the fatality, beyond the letters (which establish some degree of emotional engagement with the creature) and circumstantial murmurings from the neighbours to the effect that he had been seen hanging round in the weeks preceding. It's not a prosecution that any sensible lawyer would attempt. But the rumour that Turnbull had strangled the cat quickly gained currency – particularly among the legal community, where, thanks to his impertinent weekly *Bulletin* column on matters of the law, Turnbull was thought something of an upstart.

In 1981 the *National Times* published a small gossip item by Richard Ackland, who in the course of some observations about Mr Turnbull's candidacy for

Liberal pre-selection in the federal seat of Wentworth, wondered archly what the cat-lovers would make of him. Mr Turnbull's writ arrived very quickly, and after a hurried powwow involving Miss Watson, Mr Ackland and the Fairfax-retained barrister Neil McPhee, the matter was settled in Mr Turnbull's favour, with modest damages. Several years later, the *Sydney Morning Herald* journalist Mark Westfield was incautious enough to add the sobriquet "Cat Strangler" to Turnbull's name in print. Again, Turnbull intervened quickly and secured a settlement. The matter has never been to court, and the speed of the settlements suggests that it never will; as a cold case, the whole thing is pretty hopeless.

Canadian media magnate Conrad Black repeated the rumour in his autobiography, *A Life In Progress*. (It must be remembered that this work was published in 1993, which was well before Mr Black's life progressed as far as his most infamous residential address, Florida's Coleman Federal Correction Complex, where he served thirty-seven months for fraud and went by the name Inmate 18330-424). The book's Australian edition restrains itself to the prim recollection that "Malcolm's fugues were notorious, such as the time (as a young single man) he allegedly punctuated an altercation with a friend by disposing of her cat." The version in the book's American edition, however, is so wildly inaccurate that it demonstrates just how intricate the embroidery of this tale has become.

"Malcolm's fugues were notorious," reads the unbowdlerised account enjoyed by residents of the more permissive defamation code in the United States of America. "Such as the time he allegedly punctuated an altercation with a friend by sneaking into her home late at night and putting her kitten into the freezer, transforming a frisky pet into a well-preserved corpse."

Meanwhile, over the years the cat has assumed a legendary status far in excess of its humble breeding. In 2008 the departing *Sydney Morning Herald* columnist Alan Ramsey used one of his final columns to present a cautious version of "The Cat."

Ramsey quoted from the for-Australian-eyes edition of Black's book, and cited his artist colleague Ward O'Neill's drawing of Turnbull during his 2004 struggle for the seat of Wentworth.

"It showed Turnbull in his dressing gown holding a coffee mug bearing the image of a cat, with a cat rubbing affectionately against his leg. Political aficionados with long memories understood," Ramsey recalled.

Businesspeople and journalists understood, too. For years among Turnbull's army of detractors in Sydney, the cat story was retold with varying degrees of hysterical exaggeration. It used to function as a kind of identifying mark; you knew exactly where someone stood on Turnbull depending on whether they tried to tell you the story.

"The Cat" became a piece of eastern-suburban folklore. When Turnbull represented Packer through the "Goanna" affair, the satirist Max Gillies appeared as Packer, with a stocking pulled over his head; his routine contained a reference to cats, which would have made sense only to the initiated.

"Perhaps ... Malcolm is really a pussycat," mused the broadcaster Phillip Adams, in a 1991 profile of Turnbull.

At Fairfax, Turnbull's early hypersensitivity gave the story an untouchable status as one that cannot even be mentioned without inviting a "QCs at dawn"-style shootout. As I prepared to ask Turnbull about it, I wondered if he would fly into a rage or call in a lawyer. To my surprise, he laughed.

"All completely untrue!" was his smiling response. "No cat has died at my hands."

Turnbull said he remembered the cat, which he thought "got run over by a car. Someone, either maliciously or in jest, started the rumour and it was one of those things – sometimes the most outrageous and false things get the most currency." He said he could not remember writing any letters, but does remember the rumours spreading quickly. "At the time, I was working at the *Bulletin*. I was very upset about it. I regard it as a joke now."

Turnbull further recalled that Trevor Kennedy, his editor at the time, extended him some blokey reassurance. Kennedy, who used to trap rabbits as a kid, had had occasion to dispatch feral cats that found their way into his traps.

"They're buggers – they scratch you all over the place," Turnbull remembered him saying. Having noticed no such scratches on Turnbull's arms, Kennedy offered his services as an expert witness should the need arise.

Two postscripts: the episode earned Turnbull, one way or another, the lasting hatred of the late Jim McClelland, who in 1991 had this to say of Turnbull: "He's a turd. He's easy to loathe, he's a shit, he'd devour anyone for breakfast, he's on the make, he's cynical, he's offensively smug." Turnbull shrugged at the time, telling writer John Lyons that McClelland was "a bitter old man ... I'm very sorry that many years of excessive consumption of alcohol and professional disappointment have reduced what was once a sharp wit to nothing better than gutter abuse."

The Fairfax writer who drew the second round of litigation over The Cat, Mark Westfield, went on to prosper and very evidently patched up his relationship with Turnbull, who in 2009 hired him as his press secretary.

Renaissance Man

The writer Tom Keneally says Turnbull – with whom he has a warm if slightly scarred relationship dating back two decades to the birth of the Australian Republican Movement – is driven by a genuine feeling of obligation to spread his good fortune around.

"I always felt that he was, particularly in the late 1980s and early 1990s, a minority among the new rich in that he had the feelings of *noblesse oblige*," Keneally told me. "He wouldn't be out of place as a Venetian Doge."

And there is indeed something of the Italian Renaissance about Turnbull, preposterous as that sounds. He and his wife, Lucy, are compulsive givers to charities, hospitals and church enterprises. They have donated more than $1 million to the Sydney Children's Hospital. When the renovation of the Lodge veered over budget in 2015, the Turnbulls kicked in $160,000 of their own money. Turnbull is a patron of the arts, classically libertarian in his political tendencies and imbued with a passionate love of language. His sense of his own obligation to society is sincere.

The painter Lewis Miller was commissioned by Lucy and Malcolm Turnbull in 1994 to paint portraits of the family. Miller spent a week with the Turnbulls on the farm at Scone.

Miller chose to depict Malcolm and Lucy in close profile on two separate canvases, in the style of Piero della Francesca's famous diptych *Portraits of the Duke and Duchess of Urbino*. In the background, rather than della Francesca's Marche landscapes, stretches the land around Scone.

The reference is a deliberate one. The Duke of Urbino – Federico da Montefeltro, known as "the Light of Italy" – was a poetry-loving, library-building sort of cove, a giver of alms to the poor and a nurturer of young artists, among them the young Raphael. The Light of Italy and his wife, Battista Sforza, ruled together over Urbino in enviable private harmony; their relationship of equality (rare for the times, particularly when you consider that the Duchess married at thirteen) is reflected in the perfect symmetry of della Francesca's beautiful work.

It is easy to see how Miller was seized by his theme. There is no question, for instance, that Lucy Turnbull is the most important person in her husband's world.

She has helped him with all the biggest deals of his life, not just as a supportive spouse but as a lawyer, businesswoman and politician in her own right. Turnbull constantly defers to his wife's judgment, citing her ceaselessly in conversation. "I have a sense of us, rather than of me," he says. "I regret every minute I am not with her. We are very, very close – in some respects we are two individuals but also we are one entity."

It should be noted as a postscript that Lewis Miller and Turnbull, the artist and patron, did not always see eye to eye. The portraits of the children – Alexander and Daisy – are still in the Turnbulls' Point Piper home, but the parents are nowhere to be seen: Malcolm and Lucy didn't like the paintings much. Miller recalls that he commenced another portrait of Turnbull for the Archibald Prize in 1995, but Turnbull – shown the work in progress – did not like it and withdrew his cooperation. Turnbull registered his disapproval with the art dealer Ray Hughes, to whose gallery Lewis was at the time attached. According to Hughes, he ran into Turnbull at a book launch and was told: "That artist of yours is no good. He's made me look like a fat, greedy bastard."

"Well, Malcolm," rasped Hughes in delighted reply, "you must remember that he is a *realist* painter." Turnbull says he has no memory of the Archibald portrait, or the encounter with Hughes.

In a funny little twist of fate, Hughes' son Evan is now standing against Turnbull as Labor candidate for the seat of Wentworth.

Turnbull isn't much for holding grudges, but he doesn't like to be the subject of an unflatteirng anecdote. He himself is a great teller of yarns, and indulges happily in the modest embroidery that all good storytellers use to enhance and beautify their repertoires. But he does not enjoy tales told by others in which he appears even faintly foolish. He has two responses to such stories, when confronted with them: Fight or Forget. Either he argues the toss about the exact circumstances of the anecdote itself, or he claims to have no memory of the incident whatsoever.

It is as if he cannot bear anyone else to draft a version of his history; it's no coincidence that he has written his own books about the *Spycatcher* case and the republic campaign, two of the most public chapters of his life.

Still, as Nietzsche wrote at the age of forty-two in his iconoclastic work *Beyond Good and Evil*, "egoism is the very essence of the noble soul." Or as Malcolm Turnbull (at nineteen) wrote in student newspaper *Honi Soit*: "One has to be somewhat egoistic to achieve anything, given the jealous, carping nature of the mass of humanity." This grand pronouncement formed the third paragraph of an extremely grand 1974 article about Gough Whitlam by Turnbull, in which he suggested that the then prime minister had "fallen into the classic trap of the egomaniac." Whitlam had, posited the young Turnbull, surrounded himself with yes-men and as a result become out of touch. "This childish business of putting his leadership on the line every time he doesn't get his own way is straight out of the Elysée Palace in the days of de Gaulle," harrumphed the teenager. "Me or the wilderness? Well, de Gaulle said it once too often, for he had forgotten, in 1969, that everyone is dispensable. France and even the ALP will outlive their heroes of the moment." You get a pretty strong whiff here of what the student Turnbull might have been like – confident, opinionated, full of the heartbreaking assuredness of youth.

There is a difference between egoism and egotism; it's a slightly porous distinction and much-blurred by common usage, but certainly worth considering. Egoism is a philosophical doctrine, subscribers to which believe that self-interest provides not only the motive for all conscious action, but the valid end of such action. Egotism, on the other hand, is defined by the *Merriam-Webster* dictionary as "excessive use of the first person singular personal pronoun" or "the practice of talking about oneself too much." Turnbull is certainly guilty of the second, but the first? That is a much harder call to make.

The business of the sudden switch-offs is something that colleagues do notice, and for his critics the irresistible conclusion is that Turnbull is only interested in one half of any conversation – his half. I suppose the most charitable explanation is that his considerable brain, like a shark, must remain in constant motion or perish.

The etymology of words is a particular fascination. Turnbull has a merchant trader's smattering of languages, born of his business travel in the 1980s and '90s and his innate fascination with words. He says that as a schoolboy he spoke "quite fluent, but vilely accented" French. In conversation, he regularly uses Yiddish expressions. And he did deliver a short speech in Russian, early in his first term as Member for Wentworth, at the Russian Jewish community's Chanukah celebration on Bondi Beach.

"How wonderful it is to be here, rather than at the beach resort of Odessa," he began his remarks, as Russian speakers in the crowd laughed and local officials looked puzzled. Not content simply with speaking Russian, Turnbull then executed an ambitious inside joke. "The wonderful thing about Bondi, as opposed to Odessa, is that you can be confident that all your personal belongings will be safe!" he said, facetiously – and still in Russian. The joke, which would have been comprehensible only to a

Russian speaker familiar with both Bondi and Odessa, is that you are roughly 100 per cent likely to have your bag nicked at Bondi if you are ever so incautious as to leave it unguarded for a millisecond.

There's something magpie-like about Malcolm Turnbull. He collects fascinating bits of information, shiny little anecdotes, and has a prodigious mental store of detail in the policy areas which interest him. While conducting a routine Coalition meeting on the Rudd government's carbon-sink legislation during his term as Opposition leader, Turnbull asked his colleagues: "Now: what about *Eucalyptus globulus*?" Barnaby Joyce, Turnbull's long-term National Party nemesis who now – hilariously – is his deputy prime minister, called out: "Why don't you just say 'blue gum,' Malcolm?" Turnbull simply raised his eyebrows and moved on, calling next for a discussion of "*Toona australis*." Joyce interrupted again: "If you mean the red cedar, I think you'll find its new scientific name is actually '*Toona ciliata*.'" Turnbull said nothing, but soon was observed stabbing away furtively at his BlackBerry, which thanks to the miracle of communications in the modern age must swiftly have delivered the disappointing news that Joyce was in fact correct.

This story is told – not without wry affection – by one who was present. But Turnbull, when I mention the anecdote, is indignant; his "Fight" impulse sets in. He resents the idea that he is thought pretentious for using Latin names for trees. "You see, if you talk about trees a lot," he insists, "one of the difficulties is that the common names of trees vary from place to place. A swamp oak in one place might be called something different in another area. A mountain ash, or *Eucalyptus regnans*, which is called a mountain ash in Victoria, is called something different in Tasmania. Take the sugar gum, *Eucalyptus cladocalyx* ..." Turnbull continues in this vein for some minutes, piling detail upon detail until, of the original small funny story, little remains visible.

Sometimes, the depth and scope of his brain's capacity to retain detail is nonchalantly exposed. Soon after he became prime minister in September 2015, Turnbull was expostulating to his party room on some point relating to ISIS and the rise of Islamic extremism. "He said something like, 'You'd have to go back to before the Battle of the Milvian Bridge' to find a similar example of something or other," one MP remembers, sobbing with laughter. (The Battle of the Milvian Bridge was fought in the year 312 and won by the Roman emperor Constantine the Great.) "And then he wraps up and says: 'Now, are there any general remarks?' And Ewen Jones [a Queensland Liberal National MP], who is hilarious, jumps up and says, 'I was going to say the thing about the Milvian Bridge too, Prime Minister.'"

Sometimes, it's used as a weapon. In a national security briefing on intelligence and encryption, a bureaucrat recently had the unnerving experience of Turnbull's full attention; his technical knowledge swiftly overwhelmed that of the public servant, who was "demolished" by the end of the prime minister's interrogation. "He just runs rings around people," says one who witnessed the exchange.

Sometimes, it appears to be a genuine – if hysterically ill-judged – attempt to help. Back when Kevin Rudd was prime minister and Turnbull leader of the Opposition, the two men often ran into each other at major events. Turnbull – as the MP for the seat with the highest Jewish population of any in New South Wales – often fretted over Rudd's pronunciation of Yiddish terms. At one such occasion, Turnbull pulled the prime minister aside just before he was due to speak. "Listen, Kevin. It's not in my interests to help you, but you should know that Yiddish words with a 'ch' aren't pronounced like the 'ch' in 'cherry.' It's more like this." Here Turnbull produced a throaty hawking sound, as if preparing to spit, while Rudd stared at him coldly. "For example 'Chanukah' is pronounced 'Hhhhhanukah.' Just letting you know. Really, it's worth getting it right."

You can imagine how thrilled Rudd was to receive this tutorial.

The helpfulness can extend to senior public servants. A cabinet source tells the story of an Expenditure Review Committee meeting in which Turnbull and the secretary of the Treasury, John Fraser, had a disagreement about second-round effects – the indirect results of primary policy decisions. For example, if the government decides to spend a large amount of money bailing out a failing company, one second-round effect would be that the government would save money on the Centrelink payments it would otherwise have to make to the retrenched workers of that company.

The committee was discussing some policy decision or other, and its consequent economic effects.

"You can't count second-round effects," said Fraser.

"Yes, you can!" said the prime minister.

"Well, no: we don't do that," responded Fraser, firmly.

"Yes, you can. There's an academic at the University of Western Australia who writes very persuasively about it. You should give him a call! Ask him! Here. I'll find his number."

Out came the iPad as the prime minister ferreted out the contact details for the secretary of his Treasury to get a refresher course on second-round effects.

The person who told me this story loves this aspect of Turnbull: that he engages in everything. That he questions public servants and challenges them directly. That he is such a polymath. "He's interested in second-round effects. He's interested in the curator in the Peggy Guggenheim gallery in Venice. He's interested in the crop yield in New England!"

In Canberra, you are considered well-read if you've consumed everything on offer about Australian politics. If you've read about American and British politics as well, you are thought something of a don; knowledge of European politics implies the definite possibility that you might fancy yourself. George Brandis – a voracious reader – incurred roughly as much bile for his commissioning of publicly funded bookshelves to accommodate his professional library as Peter Slipper did for claiming his subscriptions to *GQ*, *Esquire* and *Sport Diving*.

But Turnbull's brain – a restless organ – is full of everything he's ever read, and his filing system works unusually well. When I think of his brain, I picture one of those complex old switchboard systems of the 1950s where incredibly efficient ladies with perfect hair dexterously plug and unplug lines, making and breaking connections at lightning speed.

The low-point of the Abbott government, for Turnbull, was certainly the attempt in May 2015 by the prime minister, under advice from immigration minister Peter Dutton, to have cabinet invest in Dutton the power to strip Australian citizenship from suspects accused of terrorism-related offences. The move – which was introduced to cabinet with no notice or documentation – would have been in breach of Australia's international treaty obligation to prevent statelessness. The proposal was defeated by spirited opposition from Julie Bishop, Malcolm Turnbull, Christopher Pyne and Barnaby Joyce. Lavish detail of the cabinet confrontation was leaked to Peter Hartcher at the *Sydney Morning Herald*.

"It was a real turning point for Malcolm," says a colleague. "He decided at that point: this man [Abbott] is a serious danger, not only to people in Australia but to Australia's reputation internationally."

Within weeks, Turnbull delivered a powerful speech to the Sydney Institute on the importance of the rule of law and the retention of crucial civil liberties even while fighting extremism. He closed with a lethal quote from Robert Menzies (when implicitly attacking another Liberal, quoting Menzies is the equivalent of an armour-piercing bullet): "The greatest tragedy that could overcome a country would be for it to fight a successful war in defence of liberty and to lose its own liberty in the process."

But privately, Turnbull's angst at the pointless-
ness of Abbott's escalating rhetorical war on "death
cults" was perfectly captured in the poem he circulated to friends, by Constantine P. Cavafy, the Greek
poet born in the Ottoman empire. Called "Waiting
for The Barbarians", it tells you all you need to know
about Turnbull's frustration: at overblown, crude
language and at the politics of fear.

> What are we waiting for, assembled in the forum?
> The barbarians are due here today.
> Why isn't anything happening in the senate?
> Why do the senators sit there without legislating?
> Because the barbarians are coming today.
> What laws can the senators make now?
> Once the barbarians are here, they'll do the legis-
> lating ...

One is reminded strongly, at this point, of Keneally's Venetian doge. Turnbull may be achingly
modern in his lifestyle, in his enthusiasms, in his
ambitions for the Australian economy. But his
instincts on matters of governance are ancient. Conservative, in the classical sense. His discomfiture with
the Abbott attempt to strip Australian suspects of
their citizenship was partly to do with its brute viola-
tions of the principles of Magna Carta. Partly to do

with the way in which the proposal came to cabinet – verbally, that is to say, rather than introduced by way of pre-circulated written submission. And partly, one senses, he found it *aesthetically* upsetting; the idea of yanking the crude levers of fear as a political tactic. The bleakness of a world in which the response to terrorism is administrative nervousness.

It is telling that Turnbull's first recourse was to language: a long speech to the Sydney Institute, a scrap from an early-twentieth-century poet.

Why Do They Hate Me?

That there are people who hate Turnbull is beyond doubt. "The Cat" is by no means the only yarn about him that's gone around over the years; it's just the most widely circulated. The rest of them tend to involve Turnbull's hairy-chested negotiating style, which has in the past included the throwing or threatened throwing of projectiles. His style of negotiation in business and law was certainly a notorious one: he never gave in, even on small details, and he would argue and wheedle and storm and bully until the other party either gave in or went away. When in business, he dispensed legal threats like confetti.

Other threats, too, from time to time. During the frenzied negotiations in 1987 over the sale of Nine to Alan Bond, Turnbull found himself toe-to-toe with the Blake Dawson partner Bill Conley, who was acting for Bond. After Bond and Packer's handshake deal, it was left to the lawyers to argue about the sale's precise terms and conditions, in a ludicrously short period of time. Negotiations grew vexed and an angry Turnbull suggested that he and Conley "settle this outside."

Conley confirmed the incident to me, but said he considered it minor – none of them had slept, he recalled, and tense moments occur in most big deals. "When you know the whole Malcolm, you're not going to be offended by his strong and direct way of dealing." The two men are friends, and Conley admires Malcolm and Lucy Turnbull's philanthropy. "Unlike some, they do not seek particular recognition but give because of their values," he said.

Tom Keneally, who received what you might call first-degree burns from Turnbull's temper when the two were thrown together during the republican debate, nevertheless remains fascinated by and fond of Turnbull.

"I've got a thing for difficult pricks, so I kind of on balance approve hugely of people like Malcolm and Germaine Greer, who have some similarities," said Keneally. "He bore fools very badly when he was younger, including myself – he was very abrasive." Keneally is a rare breed: one who has seen something of Bad Malcolm and maintains warm feelings.

Keneally is sympathetic towards the scalded ones:

Oh yes, absolutely. Though I've got to say it's not all his fault. It's also their own vulnerability. But yeah, I can understand why their reaction was like that. It was the abrasiveness, it was the knowledge – whether they saw it as smart aleckry, it was the acerbic turn of phrase. All that stuff. The word that was always used was "arrogant." And yet, I never thought of that adjective in my head. Hand on heart, I never thought of him as arrogant. I would have thought of other words – urgent, gifted, to an extent inspired. But Australia's a bad place to be inspired in.

If some people hate Malcolm Turnbull, who or what does Malcolm Turnbull hate? He is not particularly tribal, politically. How could he be, and keep a straight face? He has had as many Labor friends as Liberal, and many's the Labor voter I know who can't quite locate anything on which they completely disagree with Turnbull.

But it's deeper than that – Turnbull, for all his notorious rages and impatience, does not appear to be driven by hate. And his reaction to people who hate him isn't automatically to hate in return. It's something else entirely; something more like puzzlement.

"He's not obsessed with revenge the way nearly everybody is," was Bob Ellis's view. "He believes that he's given talents and called to service and is amazed that people can't see why he's the one."

A small example from history: in 1999, when the republican debate occupied a great deal of Canberra's brain, and Liberal MPs sorted themselves into piles marked "Yes," "No," and "Above the Fray," the Liberal Member for Parramatta, Ross Cameron, was in no doubt about which pile was his. Cameron was a monarchist, and he despised the Australian Republican Movement and by extension its lustrous leader, Malcolm Turnbull.

"The Turnbull-ARM republic we are being offered is a sop to our popular instincts," he told parliament on 30 August 1999. "It is a throwing of the scraps of democracy from the table of the elites. This is a 'We know better than you' republic."

Only days after getting this off his chest, Cameron found himself in a sticky situation of an entirely unconnected nature. As a member of parliament's prayer group, he had organised for a small group of young Aboriginal people to visit Canberra for a few days. Flights were booked, and the $5000 sponsorship from some anonymous businessman nailed down – or so Cameron thought.

At the last minute, his sponsor called to cancel the arrangement – disaster! This left Cameron in a spot, as he explained to his squash partner, Joe Hockey, over a morning game.

Hockey, a garrulous type who specialised in bringing together the needy and the benevolent, had an idea. After their showers, the pair convened in Hockey's office, where Hockey dialled Malcolm Turnbull's number.

Turnbull and Hockey were already friends. They'd met years before while Hockey was working on privatisations for the Fahey government in New South Wales. A young, friendly man with influence over large privatisation processes was, of course, of great interest to Malcolm Turnbull at that time, and the pair got to know each other well.

When Hockey telephoned for help with Cameron's little problem, Turnbull listened. "Cameron? *Ross* Cameron? Isn't he the guy who just bagged me in parliament?"

Hockey put his hand over the phone. "Did you bag Malcolm Turnbull in parliament?" he whispered to the Member for Parramatta.

Cameron looked uncomfortable – "Weee-llllll ..."

Hockey returned to the phone. "Come on, Malcolm. Have a heart?"

Turnbull laughed, stumped up the money and the trip went ahead.

This is not to say that Turnbull isn't prepared to use nuclear force against anyone who seeks to thwart him. He is – as even a cursory examination of his business and legal record makes amply clear. Bill Conley argues that Turnbull's benign attributes – generosity, charm and intelligence – make up for the flashes of anger. The problem is that Turnbull often did business at such a breakneck rate that sometimes the brutality was all his adversaries got to see.

Breaking the Rules: Costigan

In late 1982, soon after his father's death, Turnbull agreed to go to work for Kerry Packer full-time as Consolidated Press's lawyer. Struggling with bereavement and the management of Bruce's affairs, Turnbull thought in-house work would give him a more sedate lifestyle than that on offer at the Bar. But shortly after he started at Consolidated Press, he found himself defending Packer against the most vaporous of opponents. The Costigan royal commission, convened to investigate some rather colourful irregularities within the Federated Ship Painters and Dockers Union, began to hear evidence in secret about a well-known Australian businessman and his alleged involvement in drug-running, pornography and murder.

In 1984 the *National Times* published sensational case summaries from the commission, including one concerning the mystery businessman. The newspaper gave the businessman an evocative nickname: "The Goanna." Speculation about the identity of the Goanna was rife: "Packer Is The Goanna" read a piece of graffiti in Sydney's Central railway station. Packer and Turnbull thought that the leaks from within the commission were systemic, and calculated to harm Packer himself.

"Tackling Costigan by conventional means was futile and I persuaded Packer to counter-attack with a violent public attack on Costigan," is how Turnbull described his tactics four years later. Twenty-four years later, driving between Launceston and Hobart and breaking off periodically to point out striking examples of Georgian architecture, he told me the rest of the story. "We had a meeting in Kerry Packer's boardroom," he recalled. "Kerry Packer, Jock Harper, Alec Shand and Tom Hughes. We went through what we were going to do and I was very strongly of the view that he needed to counter-attack."

Turnbull, ever eager, had already written an 8000-word press release in which Packer identified himself as the Goanna and savagely refuted the shadowy allegations against him and denounced those who spread them.

"The older gents took a more conservative point of view," Turnbull remembered.

"Kerry, having listened to everyone, said: 'How long do I get for contempt?' Someone said they thought it was five years. 'Then I'll serve that concurrently with the life sentence for murder,' he said.

"There was an old lady called Enid, she ran the telex in the lobby. She typed off this long statement onto a tape, fed the tape in, and the telex coughed and spluttered. We looked at it going out, and he said: 'Oh well, the die is cast.'"

Turnbull wasn't even thirty years old. In the following days, he redoubled his efforts, appearing on television and radio on Packer's behalf. His barrister colleagues were horrified at this departure from the doughty orthodoxies of the Bar; Turnbull was no longer functioning as a legal advocate, they thought, but rather as a vastly over-educated bouncer for Packer.

So Turnbull became a solicitor instead, and further scandalised his brethren by continuing his advocacy work under those auspices.

This story alone – like many of the pulsing narratives in which Malcolm Turnbull has been involved as a principal player – would fill its own book. If I race through it here, it is purely for reasons of space.

But it is worth noting that even the opening attack against Costigan did not constitute the high-water mark of Packer and Turnbull's aggression in the case. Packer – represented by Turnbull – commenced defamation proceedings personally against Douglas Meagher QC, who was counsel assisting Costigan.

Turnbull claimed that Meagher had himself leaked the case summaries to the *National Times* via its editor, Brian Toohey. Typically, Turnbull ramped up the legal action with a series of provocative claims in the press, including an interview in which he claimed to have "significant evidence" that Meagher had leaked the documents. That evidence was never adduced: Turnbull and Packer dropped their action, and Meagher's riposte was to have the whole thing struck out as an abuse of process. Justice Hunt, finding for Meagher, delivered a crushing condemnation of Turnbull's style, saying that his statements to the media had "managed effectively to poison the fountain of justice immediately before the commencement of the present proceedings."

In the car, Turnbull was finally prepared to spell out the nature of the "incontrovertible, rolled-gold evidence" that he was loath to reveal all those years ago. The smoking gun, he says, was surveillance evidence of a rendezvous between the key players.

"There was a meeting at the Jade Lotus restaurant in Bank Place between Meagher, [journalist] Wendy Bacon and Brian Toohey," he says.

This surveillance evidence, which according to Turnbull was gleaned from an Australian Federal Police officer, was never disclosed to the court.

"We got ourselves into the position where in order to stop Hunt striking the action out we would have had to disclose the basis of our assertion" – something, he says, that would have compromised his informant, who at the time was still employed by the AFP. "There was a lot of anger among people in the law-enforcement agencies about Costigan and Meagher," Turnbull explains.

Toohey says: "I can state categorically that Malcolm Turnbull cannot possibly have any evidence that Douglas Meagher leaked those summaries to me, because he didn't."

From the Costigan affair we can draw some preliminary conclusions about the young Turnbull. The first is that he had no regard for orthodoxy, whether it be the polite (and substantially fictitious, it must be said) convention that barristers do not speak to the press, or the generally accepted view that one should exercise caution when one's client is accused of murder and drug-running in what is effectively a closed court.

This refusal to "play by the rules" is something of a lifelong pattern for Turnbull; it explains much of his success, but it also accounts for the worst of his reputation. Breaking the rules, like standing up in the theatre to get a better view, only really works if no one else is doing it. And breaking the rules, like standing up in the theatre, always causes hard feelings.

Turnbull's aggressive use of the media during the Costigan affair was felt as an affront by legal contemporaries who thought it wasn't quite cricket. His fly-in, fly-out approach to university study caused resentment among fellow students who felt that if they could be bothered to show up to lectures, so should he. And in the NSW state parliamentary press gallery, where Turnbull moonlighted as a radio, TV and print reporter whenever his busy schedule permitted, hard feelings soon developed with some colleagues. Back then, accredited press-gallery reporters had their own dining room, where long lunches would be taken, wine imbibed and war stories exchanged. There were conventions about this stuff; stories heard over lunch were off-limits.

But sometimes, to the other reporters' annoyance, these stories would bob up under Turnbull's byline in the *Nation Review*. Hostilities built, and one day when Turnbull made a snide remark to the Channel Ten reporter Paul Mullins about one of his stories, Mullins responded by punching Turnbull to the ground. Mullins, who went on to become a Macquarie Street institution, is now on good terms with Turnbull and declines to discuss the episode, of which he is not proud. But colleagues of the time are in no doubt about what caused the friction.

The second thing we learn from Costigan is that violent tactical methods are not just something to which Turnbull will contemplate turning if sufficiently provoked. It's not enough to say that Turnbull is prepared to play hard-ball. He *prefers* to play hard-ball – that's the point. It is impossible to rid oneself entirely of the suspicion that Turnbull enjoys the intrigue – the hurling of grenades, the hot denials of drug smuggling, the gathering of surveillance detail on prominent QCs and newspaper editors. Is it any surprise that within two years Turnbull was off on a spy adventure?

Boy's Own Adventure: Spycatcher

When Turnbull set up his own legal practice in 1986 with his friend Bruce McWilliam, one of the first pieces of business he received was a mysterious brief from the barrister Geoffrey Robertson; the mission was to fight for the right of a broken-down former British intelligence officer, Peter Wright, to publish his memoir in Australia against the trenchant opposition of Her Majesty's British government, then led by Margaret Thatcher.

Turnbull scooted about the country vetting Wright and putting together an argument for the case, which had been declared unwinnable by a series of senior barristers.

Mrs Thatcher's cabinet secretary, Sir Robert Armstrong, was the vessel for the British government's staunch resistance to publication. A snowstorm of correspondence and demands for document discovery ensued, as Turnbull – assisted by Lucy – assiduously read everything he could about the spying game. Turnbull remained square-jawed in the face of the thrilling news that his phone was likely to be bugged.

He and his British colleague David Hooper, a lanky toff and old Etonian, devised complex techniques to unnerve the intelligence agencies and Mrs Thatcher's government, particularly Sir Robert Armstrong. They staged elaborately hoaxed discussions to keep the British spooks guessing.

"Is that you, Hoops?" Turnbull would bark down the phone line.

"Absolutely. I have just got back from seeing Boris. He can't get any pictures, or any clear ones."

"How clear are they?"

"Well, I don't think you can be sure it is Armstrong. Boris says it's Armstrong. Apart from the old Etonian tie on the door, there's nothing to indicate it's Armstrong."

"Can you see the mole?"

"No, can't pick that up. I'm just not sure it's Sir Bob. Even though Boris is financing the case, I don't really trust Russians."

And so on. The pair exchanged hoax faxes and delighted in thinking of new ways in which to feed red herrings to their shadowy adversaries.

"The quality of these conversations was not high and generally demonstrated a lamentably ribald lack of respect for our opponents," Turnbull later admitted. "With an eleven-hour time difference between Sydney and London, they generally occurred late either in my night or Hooper's night, and not infrequently after one of us had returned from dinner."

The *Five Go to Spy Island* feel is much enhanced by Turnbull's own account of the affair, which is enclosed within the hardboard covers of his 1988 book *The Spycatcher Trial*. Halfway through the book, for example – trial underway – Malcolm and Lucy and their chum Paul Greengrass are electrified to discover a cache of secret letters incriminating the British aristocrat Victor Rothschild in the leaking of British intelligence secrets from Wright.

An excitable three-way discussion in the Turnbull home ensues. "We need to get Peter to cough the lot on Rothschild," decides Turnbull. "We then need to make the allegation about Rothschild public. We need to stir up the Opposition in London with calls to prosecute Rothschild. The government will have to respond by saying they are going to investigate. Rothschild might defend himself by telling the truth."

"If the conspiracy is the truth," corrects Lucy (one senses that she often exercises a moderating role).

"Well, if it isn't, they should bloody well charge him," responds Turnbull hotly. "Anyway, I think we need to get the Labour Party involved ... How do we get onto [the British Labour leader, Neil] Kinnock?"

The vast majority of legal advocates would not think of contacting a politician directly during a trial in an attempt to create helpful political pressure. But our protagonist did not hesitate; within weeks, he had got through to the British Labour leader and given him a brisk set of riding instructions on how to bring down not only Armstrong, but also the British attorney-general, Michael Havers.

The record of the telephone conversation between Kinnock and Turnbull makes for brilliantly weird reading. What other conservative leader in the world is on record as having once rung up and bullied the Labour Party to bring down someone on his own side? And the funniest thing is that Kinnock really did have to be pushed hard, as Turnbull's own account of the conversation illustrates:

"In order to flush out this lie you have to humiliate Havers. You have to accuse them of legal incompetence, until all of his friends are laughing at him. No matter how mediocre a lawyer he may really be, he is the first law officer and he must have some pride."

Kinnock sounded quite alarmed. "But the real villain is the PM, not Michael. He's sick, you know. So's Rothschild for that matter. They are both old men, this business could kill them."

I was quite surprised at this touch of humanity. It was so unlike a politician to be concerned about the health of his opponents. I didn't know what to say, so I made a joke. "Oh well, Comrade, everyone has to make sacrifices for the revolution. Why not start with Havers and Rothschild?" I heard a gasp at the other end.

Kinnock got into trouble just for taking the call from Turnbull; the Australian lawyer was considered something of a public enemy to Britannia at the time. One MP later said that it was as if Kinnock had, during the Falklands War, rung the Argentinian military dictator General Galtieri for a quick chat about tactics.

Turnbull won the case for his client, generating global sales for *Spycatcher* of more than a million copies. To the publisher's great relief, the marketability of the book survived Turnbull's central courtroom defence of it, which was that every disclosure of significance made within the Spycatcher's pages had already been published in existing spy books or in the course of televised interviews. Another victory for Turnbull, who once again had proved himself to be a devastating combination of lawyer, barrister, private investigator, public-relations guru and political strategist.

Adventures in Patricide: Tourang

There are two lessons to be learnt about Malcolm Turnbull from his role in the receivership, sale and restructure of the Fairfax media empire in the early 1990s. The first is that Turnbull has limitless determination. The second is that he is virtually unbullyable.

When the sun rose on this new decade, it found Malcolm Turnbull already farcically hyper-involved in the Australian media landscape. To chart his interests properly, you would need a wall-sized sheet of butcher's paper and a good supply of coloured crayons, such was the sinuous interconnection of his various activities.

He was a principal, with Nicholas Whitlam and the former NSW Labor premier Neville Wran, in a merchant bank established with the financial backing of Kerry Packer and the FAI boss Larry Adler. Turnbull was eventually to fall out with three of those men: Whitlam, and the late Messrs Packer and Adler. One businessman I talked to told me of sitting next to Adler at an insurance-industry lunch, where Adler said of the bank's principals, in his thick Hungarian accent: "Wran is absolutely charming. Whitlam is very lazy, and Malcolm is absolutely crazy."

Here are the highlights of Turnbull's media entanglements from the year 1990. He was a board member at the Nine Network. He advised Westpac on the handling of its $250 million loan to Channel Ten, which made the bank Ten's principal secured creditor. He advised Hudson Conway on its bid for the Seven Network. And he had already taken nearly $10 million in fees from Fairfax, being for extensive advice to the doomed Warwick Fairfax, including a recommendation to sell the *Age* newspaper, which Fairfax ignored.

Viewed at history's clarifying distance, this all looks ridiculous – just too *much*. But Turnbull at the time was calmly unmoved by allegations that he was too involved.

"All conflicts can be resolved by full disclosure," he told the *Sydney Morning Herald* in 1990. "You say 'Here are all the details, are you happy with it?' And if the client says it's okay, then you're absolved."

To the *Age* he explained that he had a low boredom threshold. "It's all a question of what people need. In order to remain amused, I probably need a high degree of adrenalin and excitement, all that sort of stuff."

Turnbull had an optimistic approach to conflict-of-interest issues even as a young man. In the course of writing his legal column for the *Bulletin* in 1981, for instance, he praised a book called *The Reasonable Men: Trollope's Legal Fiction* for its insights into the British novelist's background in the law.

"It is refreshing, if not surprising, to find someone who maintains that that most pellucid of novelists, Anthony Trollope, owed his literary style to the law," Turnbull wrote approvingly, without mentioning that the author of the work in question, while quite possibly an authoritative voice on Trollope and the law, was also his mother. To call this unorthodox conduct on the part of a reviewer would be understating the matter. But the orthodoxy of disclosure, in this instance, was yet another rule that Turnbull felt he could ignore.

Perhaps we can forgive his filial enthusiasm. After all, what are the odds that your mother will write a book whose subject matter so perfectly lends itself to a mention in your specialised column? He would have found it much harder to disguise a plug for Mum's next book, which was called *The Old Brown Dog: Women, Workers and Vivisection in Edwardian England.*

Not everyone shared Turnbull's sanguine view about managing conflicts of interest between his TV responsibilities, needless to say. In late 1990, Turnbull – working for Westpac – designed a restructure plan for Channel Ten which included a battle plan for dealing with the station's management and its chief executive, Steve Cosser. One of the features of the proposal was Turnbull's idea of circumventing Cosser's expected intransigence by broadcasting Ten's signal, if need be, from the Nine Network's transmitters.

Elements of the plan leaked, creating a widespread belief that Turnbull's management plan involved a low-cost network whose market share would shrink to 10 per cent of the viewing audience. The disclosure of Turnbull's involvement and the leaking of elements of his proposal drew protests from the then communications minister, Kim Beazley, and the chairman of the Trade Practices Commission, Bob Baxt. Baxt issued a warning to Westpac that it should keep Turnbull at arm's length from Ten.

Baxt's letter went out on a Friday. On Sunday, he travelled to Sydney with his wife (the couple lived in Melbourne), to visit his wife's mother. To Baxt's utter astonishment, lunch was interrupted by an angry Malcolm Turnbull, calling the mother-in-law's home phone.

"How did you get this number?" asked Baxt.

"I can get anyone's number if I want to," came Turnbull's chilling reply.

At about this point in the Ten proceedings, Westpac began to develop understandable concerns about the level of political and regulatory fire being drawn by its talented young consultant. With the threat of injunction from the Trade Practices Commission, and the enmity of the federal government, who could blame the bank? Westpac chairman Eric Neal called Turnbull in for a meeting; Turnbull believes that Neal intended to stand him down from the Ten receivership.

"Eric," said Turnbull, with menace. "If you throw me over the gunwale, I will take you by the throat and you will be coming with me. I have done nothing without your authority."

This is the Turnbull from all the old stories. The Turnbull who stops at nothing, who threatens and cajoles and heavies his way into what he wants. The man whose indefatigability in pursuit of his objectives does not vary according to the magnitude or importance of the objective; if he wants something, he will do absolutely anything to get it.

"Oh, I don't think any of us have any illusions about Malcolm," said one of his supporters in the Liberal party room, cheerily. "I mean, he would destroy you if you got in his way and think absolutely nothing of it."

The battle for Fairfax is the best demonstration of this. Turnbull, still close to Packer but established in his own merchant bank, watched with interest the deterioration of the Fairfax media company's fortunes as it floundered towards receivership in 1990. There was a profit to be made from the company, once the damage from Warwick's ineptitude had been contained. But how?

Like a dingo prowling the perimeter fence, Turnbull probed here and there for weak points. And found one.

Fairfax was, by late 1990, in serious hock: $1.1 billion to the banks and $450 million to a US-dominated collection of companies holding subordinated debentures; these parties went by the unencouraging title of "junk-bond holders." By late 1990, Fairfax had embarked upon the delicate task of breaking the news to these bond holders that perhaps they and their money should start to make their goodbyes.

But Turnbull offered himself to the junk-bond holders as an advocate, prepared to accept a small salary and expenses on the promise of a healthy success fee should he prevail on their behalf. The Fairfax board, knowing Turnbull's addiction to litigation, was horrified at the prospect of such a partnership: a complicated courtroom fight between Fairfax and its own creditors, the directors reasoned, would decimate confidence in the company and repel buyers.

On Wednesday 31 October 1990, Fairfax director Bill Beerworth convened a meeting with some of the bond holders in the LA office of their law firm, Coudert Brothers. He was there in the hope of dissuading them from appointing Malcolm Turnbull. But as he spoke, the office door kept opening to admit more of the bond holders, most of whom were far from happy with Fairfax. Harsh words were exchanged. Beer-worth began to hand around newspaper clippings about Turnbull – reports of his conflicting media interests and closeness to Packer, of the government's reservations about his role in Channel Ten, and so on.

As this small-scale leafleting took place, the door was once more thrown open and Turnbull himself marched in. He stood for a while enjoying Beer-worth's discomfiture, then added his voice to the hostile chorus.

A nasty, uncomfortable scene. But this is a defining characteristic that Turnbull brought to business and the law: he doesn't mind nasty scenes.

And in the end, of course, the prospect of being represented by an aggressive, merciless, cheeky and bargain-priced Australian advocate was more attractive to the junk-bond holders than the prospect of being propelled politely into penury by Fairfax. They signed Turnbull up on the spot. Now the dingo had his chink in the fence.

And he prised it open using his favourite tool: litigation. On behalf of the bond holders, Turnbull commenced legal proceedings within four months against Fairfax and its bankers for misleading and deceptive conduct, claiming that the company had been overly optimistic in its projections when touting for loan funds.

Now, a frenzied exchange of writs-at-ten-paces is not unusual at this level of business. And it was certainly not unusual for Turnbull, who as we know from both the Costigan and the *Spycatcher* episodes regards the court system as an arena for contests of intellect and strategy. But this particular act of litigation imbued Turnbull and the junk-bond holders with a special significance in the great struggle for Fairfax that was about to begin: it gave them a position of relevance.

"Sitting back and watching the banks sell Fairfax and shut out his clients was an option Turnbull was not prepared to entertain," wrote Colleen Ryan and Glenn Burge in their detailed account of the Fairfax affair, *Corporate Cannibals*. "For Turnbull, there is nothing worse than being ignored. If no one would deal with him, Turnbull had to make sure that he was a force to be reckoned with."

Turnbull, having encouraged his clients to commence the litigation, was the only person who could call it off. Seeing as Fairfax was much more valuable as a going concern than as a ravaged, post-litigation hulk, his ability to make the litigation go away took on a quantifiable market value.

On one construction, this is a stunningly effective legal manoeuvre. On another, it's not entirely unlike the pest exterminator who first releases a bushel of cockroaches into a house, then knocks at the door offering fumigation for a fee. For the Fairfax bankers, the litigation contained an additional and very bitter pill: Turnbull's own firm, working for Fairfax in 1988, had made valuations not dissimilar to those over which Turnbull was now suing.

"*Chutzpah*," a word Turnbull uses often, is – as he once wrote – "best defined as the characteristic of a man who kills both his parents and then throws himself on the mercy of the court on the basis that he is an orphan."

But *chutzpah* is a pretty good term to describe Malcolm's most striking attribute in business, too. *Institutionalised shamelessness* would also come close.

*

Turnbull's tactics tended to be warmly supported by those on whose behalf they were exercised. Eric Neal, veteran of Turnbull's threats at Westpac, is now Sir Eric, and has done a stint as governor of South Australia.

"He was widely sought-after," recalls the former viceroy admiringly of Turnbull. "His results were always very good."

Kerry Packer, Peter Wright and the American junk-bond holders in Fairfax must certainly have appreciated the wholeheartedness with which Turnbull was prepared to go into battle on their behalf.

Here was a man who would cheerfully make enemies among his own peers while serving a client: a rare quality, particularly in the cosy confines of the Australian legal community. There must be great comfort in finding oneself represented by an individual of superior cunning who, moreover, doesn't give a toss if his efforts on your behalf get him invited to fewer golf games. It's only those on the receiving end who moan about breach of convention, or lack of collegiality.

But given Turnbull's rapacious appetite for work, the odds in the '80s and '90s were that if you were involved in media or certain business circles in Sydney, you would probably find yourself pitted against him at some point. Hence the considerable ranks of Malcolm veterans who are wary of him.

"People have always had strong views about me, either positive or negative," he told *Good Weekend* equably in 1988, aged thirty-three. "You don't have to be very successful, contentious or different to be resented in this country. Some people are jealous of almost anybody. You just get on with your life and realise that in terms of business, success doesn't depend on whether people think you're a nice bloke or not."

Well, not when you're in business, maybe.

By dint of ceaseless nagging, coaxing, blustering and persistence, Turnbull parlayed his bond holders' interests into a seat at the table of a most influential bidding consortium, which included Mr Kerry Packer and Mr Conrad Black. Packer, Black and Turnbull met at London's Savoy Hotel on 3 June 1991 to seal the agreement, which included an undertaking from Turnbull's bond holders that they would deal with no other bidders. They called the consortium Tourang.

But the group struggled to prevail, partly due to the public suspicion of Packer's interventionist tendencies as a proprietor, and partly because Tourang did not have quite the rails run it expected in Canberra, where a divisive leadership transition from Hawke to Keating was eroding the influence of the Packer intimate Graham Richardson, of whom much had been hoped. Fairfax journalists rallied against the prospect of Packer's involvement. Word of "The Cat" was whispered around the newsrooms.

"Why do the journos hate me?" Turnbull asked the ABC's Quentin Dempster, having invited him in for a cup of coffee and some advice at the height of the journalists' campaign. Dempster had to explain that it was his links to Packer that caused suspicion in many quarters.

Within the Tourang ranks, fissures emerged between some of the gargantuan personalities involved. Trevor Kennedy, the Packer intimate, former rabbit trapper and good friend to Turnbull, was ejected. Packer grew close to a pair of American advisers who told him that Turnbull's continued presence on the Tourang team was a threat to its viability. Turnbull expected a loyal defence from his old boss but – finding none – quickly swallowed his hurt feelings and switched tactics with an extraordinary display of mercurial cunning.

It's well known that Packer's presence on the Tourang consortium was skewered sensationally in November 1991 by the leaking of some notes, made by Trevor Kennedy upon his arrival in Tourang, that demonstrated Packer's intentions towards Fairfax to be distinctly more interventionist than his bellicose public avowals gave regulators to believe. Years later, it was reported that Turnbull himself was the shadowy figure who slid into Australian Broadcasting Tribunal chairman Peter Westerway's car one night in a quiet North Sydney street and slipped him a paper bag full of diary notes.

But it wasn't until 2009, when I was in a car in Tasmania interviewing Turnbull seventeen years after the Tourang events, that he at last personally supplied the narrative of that spectacular denouement.

"It was fairly tense," he began, somewhat superfluously, when I asked him about it. "I regarded what Kerry was doing as absolutely ... it was not only stupid but it was contrary to everyone's interests. And he was taking the view that because he was bigger and richer than me, he could run me into the ground. So I rang Kerry Packer and I had a major row with him. I said, 'If you want to do this, this is it. This is the end. There is no stepping back from this. This is war.'"

Asked about the particulars of his threat to Packer, Turnbull's answer was straightforward: "I told him I'd get him thrown out of the deal. I never make threats I don't carry out." But he had to be pressed quite hard to vouchsafe the exact nature of Packer's response.

"He was fairly upset about it," is the way he put it at first. Pressed further, he said: "I can't recall." He even lapsed briefly into Italian in an attempt to change the subject – "*Avanti, sempre avanti*! (Onward, ever onward!)" But eventually, he spelled it out.

"Kerry was, um, Kerry got a bit out of control at that time," he said. "He told me he'd kill me, yeah. I didn't think he was completely serious, but I didn't think he was entirely joking either. Look, he could be pretty scary."

Once the disclosure was out, Turnbull warmed to the narrative task.

He did threaten to kill me. And I said to him: "Well. You'd better make sure that your assassin gets me first because if he misses, you better know I won't miss you." He could be a complete pig, you know. He could charm the birds out of the trees, but he could be a brute. He could be like that. But the one thing with bullies is that you should never flinch. My father taught me that if someone threatens you with violence, you never, ever succumb. The minute you do, someone will say: "Oh, so-and-so threatened to belt him and he buckled."

Packer, it has been reported, did like to keep a firearm close at hand. The prospect of Australia's richest man flattening himself in a doorway in order to unload a few rounds into Turnbull on his way back from the gym does stretch the imagination somewhat. But there is no doubt that the late Mr Packer was full of surprises. As Turnbull put it, he was scary.

He was a difficult, mercurial guy. He could be quite capricious. I had a row with him once, about something he was doing – I can't remember what. I said to him: "Kerry, this is a very bizarre way to run a business." He leaned back and said: "Ah. But what you overlook is that I am a very bizarre person."

The die being cast, Turnbull went about his business and delivered the papers to Westerway on the evening of Sunday, 25 November 1991. Westerway, even when told of Turnbull's admission, would not confirm the identity of the man who slipped into the passenger seat of his car just after dusk on a street in Kirribilli, near the Ensemble Theatre, beyond saying that he was a public figure known to him, who had telephoned earlier in the day.

"He rang me and said that he had some material to give me which was of importance or relevance to the inquiry," recalls Westerway. "He was not prepared to come into the office. So we met on a street down the back of Kirribilli – near a theatre in Kirribilli down the back."

Westerway's source told him, as he handed over the copy of Kennedy's notes, that "he, his wife and family were all at risk."

"He had a genuine apprehension," Westerway says of his informant. "Whether it was well-based or not, I have no way of knowing."

On Tuesday, Westerway announced an Australian Broadcasting Tribunal inquiry into Tourang. And on Thursday, Packer withdrew from the consortium. Turnbull told me he only regretted one action at that time: telling Lucy, who was understandably horrified by Packer's threat.

After telling me the story in 2009, though, Turnbull developed significant remorse. He called me many times, asking me to take his words off the record. He didn't want to cause grief for the Packer family. Even now, six years later, he adduces that interview as evidence of why politicians should never talk to journalists when they're tired. One of his favourite phrases, as he contemplates a long election campaign, is: "Don't kill the candidate." He is determined to sleep well and stay rested.

Conrad Black, who remained in the Tourang consortium and went on to win Fairfax without Turnbull or Packer, later wrote of Turnbull that he was "an intelligent, attractive and articulate man, who sometimes has considerable difficulty maintaining his self-control against an onslaught of unimaginable compulsive inner tensions and ineluctable ambitions."

Turnbull and Black spoke after the tumultuous phone call with Packer.

"Black rang me, to try and persuade me [to resign]," Turnbull recalls. "I said, 'Conrad, if you want to be an assassin, you have got to get blood on your hands.'

"He said to me, and I thought it was quite a good answer: 'You don't just want me to have blood on my hands, you want my bloody fingerprints on the dagger.'"

If he feels he is being bullied, Turnbull will respond with full belligerence and no qualms whatsoever. His business career is full of lavish overreactions to threat. Truly, this is a man who would wear a howitzer to a knife fight.

"Well, he started it," is his conclusion on the Packer business. "What do you do? It's like punching somebody and being surprised when they hit you back. I've dealt with a lot of brutes in my time. Jimmy Goldsmith, Conrad Black, [Robert] Maxwell. Rupert, on many occasions. I've dealt with bullies in the corporate world all my life."

There is something of a teenager's braggadocio in Turnbull's defiance of power; something of the paranoiac, too. The language he has traditionally used – much talk of "retaliation," "hitting back," "crushing" – is itself laced with aggression. For decades, he has had a crash-bang-wallop approach to conflict, and what appears to be an almost hardwired, violent response to any threat of subordination. He seems perennially to be alert for signs that someone is about to exert their power and influence to dominate him. The defence reflexes of that kid – the unhappy one in the boarding school at eight years old, beaten up for his defiance of bigger boys, and yet not backing down – have survived into adulthood, and hardened into habit.

"No judge is ever going to run over the top of me. Nobody is going to bully me," he told *Good Weekend* in 1988. "I will not respond to bullying from Mr Cousins, or bullying from any other person who cares to try and bully me," he said in 2007 in response to a campaign by businessman Geoff Cousins against one of Turnbull's decisions as environment minister.

Turnbull's strong public views about bullies do raise a smile in some quarters. For all his identification with journalists, Turnbull is notorious for going over their heads in the event of dispute. When the ABC journalist Sarah Ferguson undertook a profile on Turnbull for the ABC show *Four Corners* in mid-2008, the then shadow treasurer was initially cooperative but developed reservations about the advisability of being seen to promote himself when tensions within the party were so delicately balanced. As negotiations continued, Turnbull emailed the ABC managing director, Mark Scott, to complain about Ferguson.

When Miranda Devine wrote a *Sydney Morning Herald* column critical of Turnbull in 2007, he complained directly to the newspaper's then editor, Alan Oakley. And in a speech to a 2009 Liberal Forum event hosted by the then News Limited CEO John Hartigan and attended by several News Limited editors, Turnbull made extensive mention of his closeness to Murdoch. At News, where proximity to the Sun King carries its own privileges, the implicit message to the editors was clear: *Don't mess with me, because I may be able to mess with you.*

Incidentally, one of the stories Turnbull told that night – the tale of how he met Murdoch – is a great example both of Turnbull's *chutzpah* and of the strange way the universe has of occasionally bending to suit him.

Turnbull's overseas holiday in Christmas 1976 was eventful in many ways. He interviewed Enoch Powell. He stayed on and off with Bob Ellis, who was living in Camden. And he received a telegram from Trevor Kennedy, editor of the *Bulletin*, offering him a full-time job. Turnbull was fired by enthusiasm and ambition. He decided to go to New York, where Rupert Murdoch had just bought *New York Magazine* in a hostile takeover, and file a story for Channel Nine about Murdoch's conquest.

Turnbull organised a freelance camera crew and raced about recording interviews. At one point, he was recording a piece to camera next to a newsstand when he noticed the Australian art critic Robert Hughes wandering by. Turnbull collared him and interviewed Hughes on camera; neither man was aware that within five years Turnbull would be married to Hughes's niece, or that a long way down the track Turnbull would convert part of his home into a virtual hospital ward to accommodate the recuperating Hughes after a dreadful car accident. But Turnbull had great trouble getting to Murdoch himself.

"I kept on ringing and ringing and ringing the *New York Post*," says Turnbull. (The *Post* was already owned by Murdoch, and functioned as his New York headquarters.) "He was not giving interviews to anybody. So I just started dialling one extension after another. And finally I fluked it – I got through to the extension on Rupert Murdoch's desk. I said something like 'Jeez, Rupert Murdoch. You've got to help me out. I'm completely screwed!'" Murdoch, presumably impressed by the reporter's persistence, consented to an interview, and Turnbull's bacon was saved.

Just as there's something awe-inspiring about Turnbull's relentless pursuit of Murdoch, there's something spectacular about his defiance of Packer. You have to remember that this is a man barely anyone ever crossed – not this flagrantly, anyway.

Perhaps the most famous footage of Packer is of his quasi-tyrannical appearance before a bank of politicians during parliament's Print Media Inquiry during the Fairfax upheaval. From the moment he introduced himself – "Kerry Francis Bullmore Packer. I appear here reluctantly" – Packer's dominance of the room was apparent, even when viewed through the moderating eye of television. Irascible, wary, reptilian, he wheeled and lunged at his questioners in an unconscious but almost comically perfect vindication of the *National Times'* choice of nickname for him in 1984.

"I think you have a damn hide," Packer snapped at one MP. "I do not intend to cooperate with you in the blackening of my character," he informed another.

Packer was before the inquiry to answer questions about his intentions for Fairfax, but it was a question about his relationship with the Australian Taxation Office that elicited the most memorable quote of the afternoon.

"Of course I minimise my tax," he growled. "Anybody in this country who does not minimise tax wants his head read. I can tell you that as a government you are not spending it so well that we should be donating extra."

Packer was a reclusive character. He existed almost as a fable in this country; a terrifying but elusive miasma of whispered tales in which he ate whole companies alive, or flipped some Texan oilman for $60 million. The rare public appearance before the committee cemented a common view of Packer: here was a man at the peak of his powers, before whom even the parliament quailed, and for whom the payment of tax was a substantially avoidable inconvenience.

Keep in mind, Turnbull's crazy-brave defiance of him took place just seventeen days after that appearance. The Kerry Packer that so dominated a room of politicians of both stripes is the same man that Turnbull set out quite deliberately to goad and destroy.

As is so often the case with Malcolm Turnbull, there is a postscript. Packer and Turnbull, furious with each other, did not speak for two years, although Turnbull spoke to Ros Packer from time to time. Finally, the two men effected a rapprochement: lunch in the back room at Beppi's, a tycoon-infested East Sydney Italian restaurant. The rift finally seemed healed a year before Packer died, when one summer night the ailing mogul and his wife made a rare excursion for dinner down the road to the Turnbulls' place.

Malcolm Turnbull went to work for Packer when his own father died. And in the brilliant and cantankerous mogul, he found something of a replacement father. Hard, then, for either man to get over the events that passed between them; the act of abandonment from Packer, the responding act of near-patricide from Turnbull.

But get over it they did. The two couples sat out on the terrace with a handful of friends until three in the morning, without a trace of rancour; Lucy Turnbull remembers it as a warm and happy goodbye.

The Enormous Crocodile

Malcolm Turnbull's life is full of trailing creepers that connect the terrain of politics to other, more exotic destinations. Conversations with him are the same. One day we were talking about the Australian edition of the *Spectator* and whether it would last. Turnbull said he thought it would (he is enthusiastic about new publications, as a rule, and isn't fibbing when he says he retains a passion for journalism).

"I once tried to buy the *Spectator*," he added, almost as an afterthought.

A furtive check reveals that, yes, he did. Charles Moore, editor of the *Spectator* from 1984 to 1990, wrote in 2003 about his encounter with Turnbull nearly twenty years earlier:

One dark winter afternoon, I returned from parliament to my office and found Malcolm Turnbull sitting on the sofa. Turnbull was soon to become famous as the lawyer in the *Spycatcher* case, and, later, as one of the leaders of the unsuccessful republican movement in Australia, but at this time he was Kerry Packer's man of business, and I had never heard of him. He told me that Packer wanted to buy *Spectator* (he omitted the definite article) and that the deal would be through next week. I felt very depressed and asked Turnbull why Mr Packer wanted the paper. He thought for a moment and then said: "Well, Kerry's not only motivated by greed." He then seemed to reflect that he had done his boss an injustice, for he added: "Well, not all the time, anyway." Luckily, this coincided with the Goanna Affair, a complicated scandal in Australia in which Mr Packer was somehow involved. As a result, the deal did not happen.

Four years later, according to Moore's account, he received a call from Rupert Murdoch.

"I've just been offered the *Spectator* by Malcolm Turnbull," the mogul announced.

"I hadn't realised it was Malcolm's to sell," grumped Moore, who in any event repelled Murdoch's advance. Turnbull, for his part, has no memory at all of trying to interest Murdoch in the magazine.

The *Spectator* episode gives us an insight into what Malcolm Turnbull was like in business. Speculative, confident, showy, and prepared to invoke names in order to further his own plans. When asked in detail about his *Spectator* bid, Turnbull couldn't quite remember if he had even been working for Packer at the time of his approach to Moore.

"I talked to Kerry about it; Kerry wasn't that interested," he recalled. "He was sort of mildly interested. It was only worth a million quid – not a lot of money. It was a fixer-upper. Not, in any conventional terms, a serious asset."

Then he was off into another fascinating reminiscence: from 1979, when he and Packer attempted to buy London's *Times* and *Sunday Times*, then owned by the Thomson Corporation and riven with industrial strife. Turnbull himself had been a first-hand veteran of the industrial trouble.

Here's the background: Turnbull, who travelled to Britain and the United States during his university holidays in late 1975, gave a speech at the Cambridge Union while he was there. After his oration, Turnbull was thrilled to receive a handwritten note from the famed *Sunday Times* editor Harold Evans (who, thanks to the magical hand of Fate that seems perennially to hover over Malcolm Turnbull, happened to be in the audience).

The note read: "Dear Turnbull – Magnificent speech. See me in the Gray's Inn Road tomorrow. Harold Evans."

"It was like a message from God," remembered Turnbull, who delivered himself smartly to the *Times'* famed London address the next day. Evans offered him a job on the spot; Turnbull demurred, saying he needed to go home and finish his law degree.

"Don't do law," Evans told him. "Terrible things could happen. You could become a judge. Or – worse – a politician!"

Turnbull did go home, but stayed in touch with Evans, and when he returned to England and Oxford in 1978 as a Rhodes scholar, he started work at the *Sunday Times*. But the paper was so mired in industrial discord that for ten months it was not published: Turnbull and the other hacks would spend the week running around writing stories that never saw the light of day because the print unions refused to print the paper. Good rehearsal for Opposition, perhaps, but hardly fun for a keen young journalist, so eventually Turnbull resigned and took himself back to Oxford to concentrate on his studies.

But he continued to think about what could be done to break the hold of the unions. And so to 1979. Turnbull had already worked for Kerry Packer as assistant to Packer's finance director, Harry Chester, for eight months (a heady experience for the young man that involved a trip to *Playboy* headquarters to negotiate an Australian edition of the soft-porn magazine). Now he thought that perhaps Packer could buy the *Times* group and introduce a union-busting plan that would get the papers back in print.

Packer, Turnbull and Evans (for the editor was receptive to the idea) staged some initial councils-of-war in Evans' Pimlico home.

"We had a Wapping plan to deal with the unions," Turnbull remembered.

We had a very funny meeting about it at the Dorchester Hotel, working through all the logistics of getting the paper into the country, printing and distributing it. We had these partners from Linklaters telling us about the provisions of these acts and so on, and Kerry was getting frustrated. He eventually said: "Look. I'm driving the truck, right? With all the papers on the fucking back. We're coming off the ramp at the back of the building. There are all these picketers. I beep the horn. They don't get out of the way. So I lean out the window and I say, 'Can you please get out of the way?' But they don't get out of the fucking way. So I drive the truck very slowly, and I run one over. What law covers me then?" And this partner from Linklaters, very pale, stammers: "The law of m-m-m-murder!"

In 1994, when the British Labour leader Tony Blair flew across the globe to formalise the defrosting of his relationship with Rupert Murdoch's News Corporation, the mogul joked: "If the British press is to be believed, today is all part of a Blair–Murdoch flirtation. If that flirtation is ever consummated, Tony, I suspect we will end up making love like two porcupines – very carefully."

It's a good characterisation of the awkward relations between politicians and media barons. In Malcolm Turnbull, however, Australia has a leader who already has engaged in vigorous and largely unprotected congress with most of the last century's most celebrated moguls.

"I think the age of the crazy sort of flamboyant megalomaniac à la Jimmy Goldsmith, Conrad Black, to some extent Kerry Packer, is probably over," reflects Turnbull.

Which was the maddest one he ever dealt with, I ask.

"Oh, Robert Maxwell, for sure. Closely followed by Jimmy Goldsmith, followed by Conrad Black."

"You didn't have much to do with Maxwell, though, did you?"

Oh, quite a bit actually, when I was, we were, trying to get all Warwick Fairfax's debt paid off, after he'd foolishly borrowed 1.2 billion dollars and bought the family company, and he had to sell assets … One of the assets that we were considering selling was the Melbourne *Age*, for – um – eight hundred and fifty million dollars, I think it was that Maxwell was prepared to pay for it back in 1988. Wouldn't be worth anything approaching that now. It'd be worth … it might be hard to sell, I would think. On any basis, regrettably.

We were negotiating the sale of the *Age*, [in the] rather splendid surroundings of the suite imperial of the Ritz hotel in Paris and we were about fifty million dollars apart, and Maxwell said – and he had all these lawyers and bankers there, he was wanting to impress – "Mr Turnbull, I will write one figure on a piece of paper and you shall write another figure, and then, you know, if my figure is higher than yours that's what I'll pay, and if not we'll split the diff." He had this elaborate sort of thing going on, and I just thought, "This is nuts," so I grabbed him and I said, "No, Robert, you and I are just going to step into the bedroom here for a second." So we stepped into the bedroom and I closed the door and I said, "Now look, let's just cut all the bullshit – what are you prepared to pay for it?" and we struck a handshake deal. It was eight-fifty, eight-seventy five, something like that and then Warwick decided – had a change of heart, because his mother had persuaded him that he didn't need to sell the *Age* to get his debt down. If he'd done that, he would've been basically home clear, he would've owned all of the NSW papers, the *Financial Review* and no debt. But his mother said to him, "No, no, I've found this wonderful firm called Drexel Burnham Lambert, and they've got this great invention called junk bonds, which can come to your salvation." And that worked out brilliantly – that's why he ended up with absolutely nothing.

The junk-bond holders, of course, later became Turnbull's own way back into Fairfax; such are the criss-crossing threads of the Turnbull life story.

You can get to know a lot about a person by observing what sort of stories they enjoy telling most. And for Malcolm Turnbull, it's swashbuckling tales of defiance against figures of might and authority. Or cunning plots, perfectly executed.

"I've got secret plans and clever tricks!" the prime minister has been known to bellow jovially when in an especially good mood. It's a line from *The Enormous Crocodile*, a Roald Dahl story which Turnbull was fond of reading to his children.

Of his moments in office so far, easily the most triumphant for Turnbull personally was the switcheroo he pulled on the Australian Senate in March 2016. Turnbull and his lead Senate negotiator Mathias Cormann cut a deal with the Greens in February to bring forward debate on reforming the way Australians elect their senators. Both parties were keen to eliminate the quirk by which voters – lodging a vote for a minor party – could find that vote pinging around through various intricate preference deals and ultimately see it land somewhere quite different. Sex Party votes might end up with the Liberal Party. Or pro-environment votes with the Shooters and Fishers Party. The government and Greens clubbed together to outgun resistance from the Labor Party and most of the crossbenchers, who were very much the target of the legislation. It was agreed that another contentious piece of legislation – the proposed re-establishment of the Australian Building and Construction Commission – would be put off until the next session.

Paul Kelly wrote scorchingly, in the *Australian*, that the government had "mismanaged the ABCC bill. It should have been reintroduced late last year to establish the second 'failure to pass,' thereby running the bill on to the double dissolution list."

"The upshot is a mess," he chided. "The Senate has announced it will not bring forward its budget sittings, thereby creating doubt over whether, in the short time available, the Senate will consider the ABCC bill in such a way that Turnbull can justifiably include it in the list of bills when he advises the Governor-General to dissolve parliament. How can Turnbull campaign against the CFMEU during the election if the ABCC bill is not on a double dissolution list to be passed at a joint sitting post-election?"

Turnbull took everyone by surprise, however, on 22 March. Appearing in the prime minister's courtyard and – he announced that he had instructed the governor-general to call back the Senate for three extra weeks in April, where senators would be obliged either to accept the ABCC legislation or reject it, thereby forcing a 2 July double dissolution election under the new rules it had just passed. To recall parliament, Turnbull used an often-overlooked provision of the constitution, section 5.

The whole exercise involved some classic Turnbull themes. A little-known legislative provision. A stunning tactical pivot. A lengthy and elegantly worded written appeal to the governor-general. A crushing blow to someone – in this case the Greens – who had been a co-conspirator but now found the game seriously changed. ("Richard di Natale – meet Malcolm Turnbull," chuckled one Liberal with long experience of the Turnbull technique, on the day the prime minister revealed his hand. "Have fun!")

Turnbull, as previously discussed, has a terrible poker face. If he's bored, he looks bored. If he's angry, you know about it. And if he's pleased, the pleasedness emanates almost visibly off him in happy clouds. The Senate reform coup made him deeply happy; being proved to be clever is so much sweeter when, for weeks, you've been condemned as a fool. "Secret plans and clever tricks!" he declared. It was a good day in the Turnbull office.

A less successful exercise was to follow, however.

The 2014 federal budget presented by Joe Hockey and Tony Abbott contained nasty surprises for everyone from patients to pensioners, but there was one page, and one graph, that scandalised state and territory leaders. It indicated that the government planned to abandon the Gillard government's promised rates of increases to education and health spending. This decision – over ten years – would constitute a saving to the Commonwealth of $80 billion. The federal government's "$80 billion cuts to health and education" became a banner under which premiers and territory leaders gathered regardless of ideological stripe. How would the schools and hospitals of the future be funded? It was an open question.

Two premiers – Liberal Mike Baird, from New South Wales, and Labor's Jay Weatherill, from South Australia – declared themselves open to a discussion about changing the tax base. Both were prepared to countenance a rise in the rate of GST. Weatherill floated the idea of directing a proportion of federal income tax to the states, rather than having state governments beg for money, as they currently have to.

A meeting was set for 1 April – a Friday – in Canberra. Turnbull's cabinet discussed the taxation matter. A GST increase was no longer viable. No one around the table had much appetite for raising taxes federally and then just handing the proceeds to the states. Turnbull proposed a tweak to the Weatherill proposal: why not allot a proportion of income tax to the states, but give them actual responsibility for raising it too? If each state had the capacity to raise or lower taxes, then state governments would also be forced to accept the political responsibility for their decisions.

Again, it was a classic Turnbull tactic. It made neat economic sense: of course people are more careful when spending their own money than when spending someone else's. It contained an element of surprise. And it would – if successful – be a profound reform to the federation agreement, one that exerted a force towards efficiency, and would moreover not cost a cent. In these lean days, when vision is expensive and the cupboard is bare, it was an appealing idea. Cabinet agreed that Turnbull should pursue the idea.

But the execution went badly wrong. Turnbull phoned around the premiers with differing degrees of notice. Baird found out a week in advance, for example; Weatherill, on the Monday before the meeting. The premiers were surprised. Word began to leak out.

Wednesday morning found Turnbull on a train, on his way out to open a new league academy at the home of the Penrith Panthers with Fiona Scott, the Member for Penrith and subject of Tony Abbott's notorious remarks about "sex appeal." Scott was about to feature in another remarkable doorstop interview. Turnbull – over the course of his train voyage – decided that too many details were leaking out about the income-tax proposal, and the best way to regain control of the situation was to explain it himself.

And so it came to pass that the twenty-ninth prime minister of Australia found himself delivering a light tutorial on vertical fiscal imbalance and the aspirations and limitations of this nation's 115-year-old federation agreement, on a patch of grass in front of a building emblazoned with a giant panther, mid-pounce. "What we're talking about is the most fundamental reform to the federation in generations!" Turnbull enthused. "Really since the income-tax powers were ceded to the Commonwealth in the Second World War!" So many questions remained. How would this plan work? Was it indeed a solution to the problem of vertical fiscal imbalance? What role would the panther play?

Further confusion developed when Turnbull and his treasurer appeared to have a different understanding of whether premiers would be able to increase taxes, leading to higher taxes overall. No, said Morrison. Possibly, said Turnbull.

The premiers and territory leaders met at the Lodge for dinner with Turnbull the following night. It wasn't fun. The leaders – with the exception of WA premier Colin Barnett – were opposed. They felt as if they had been blindsided. Turnbull was annoyed and snippy. It was clear he wasn't going to get anywhere. "There was just no shape to it," says one leader. "No green paper, no white paper, no draft proposals. No statement of principle. Just an idea. And not a very good one at that. It was chaos."

The next morning, early, Turnbull rang Baird and gave him a blast. And later, over the drafting of the communiqué, Turnbull was cutting, suggesting that perhaps the statement could mention how "brave" certain premiers were on matters of crucial reform.

Both Baird and Weatherill – who felt they had stuck their own necks out quite significantly on the GST only to have Turnbull himself "chicken out" – were irritated by these barbs.

The proposal for a states' income tax was dead, within three days of its announcement as "the most fundamental reform to the federation in generations."

"I have had hangovers that have lasted longer than that!" tweeted Labor frontbencher Jason Clare.

The spectacle of Malcolm Turnbull ventilating a grand idea and then – within days – abandoning it was an unfortunate one. For the premiers, some of whom had approached the negotiations in a genuine spirit of good will, it seemed an extraordinary jettisoning of political capital.

"He walked into that meeting with one problem, and walked out with about four," says one COAG delegate. "I just don't think he's any good at this."

The perception of a rift between Turnbull and his treasurer was another problem, and one the prime minister's staff attempted to fix by arranging for cameras to film them leaving Parliament House together after the COAG meeting broke up on the Friday afternoon.

Awkwardly, the two men strode out together into the prime minister's courtyard and – intently tracked by the news cameras – hopped into Turnbull's car. Inside, the two men grinned queasily at each other as they buckled themselves in. "Let's not do that again," they agreed.

Turnbull was chastened by the whole affair. He rang senior colleagues over the ensuing week to apologise for his handling of the matter. For detractors, though, the whole event was a sign that Bad Malcolm was back.

Convictions

H is tactics during the closing phase of the Tourang saga were vintage Turnbull: savage, decisive, and – in a tiny way – childish. There's more than a hint of kicked-over Scrabble board about the whole thing, death threats or no death threats. It's a marvellous story and well told, as any Turnbull story invariably is. The eye goes obediently where it is drawn.

But behind the melodrama, some questions smoulder away insistently. First, there is the small but extremely piquant irony that the man who now says he feared for his life at Packer's hands in 1991 was the same man who, ten years earlier, summoned all his considerable powers of audacity and outrage to defend Packer against the suggestion that he would ever engage in violence. More significantly, there is the question of the Kennedy notes themselves and what they revealed.

The Kennedy notes skewered Packer's involvement in the Fairfax bid because they revealed that

Packer had lied to the parliamentary inquiry about the extent of his planned involvement in Fairfax. But Turnbull did not leak the notes to defend the integrity of the parliamentary record, or to strike a blow for freedom of the press.

He leaked them, according to his own graphic account, in order to teach Packer a lesson.

Had Packer not decided to cut his protégé loose, are we to assume that Turnbull would have remained peaceably complicit in the deception? In fairness to Turnbull, the leaking of the documents and the ousting of Packer from the Tourang bid did work in favour of Turnbull's clients, the junk-bond holders. With Packer out of the consortium, Tourang's was a much easier bid for the government to approve, and approve it they did, ensuring the satisfaction of the US creditors.

But this story crystallises something about Turnbull that obsesses his critics, and even bothers some of his supporters in quiet moments. Turnbull is an opportunist – a brilliant, charming, savage gun for hire. A lawyer, when all's said and done, with a considerable gift for argument combined with an unbelievable degree of persistence. His tactical abilities are all the freer for being unrestrained by excessive concern for consistency or even – in some circumstances – governing principle.

This is, unmistakably, a handy quality in business. But in politics, it becomes complicated.

The Tourang affair is the stand-out example, from Turnbull's career in business, of how far he is prepared to go to prove a point. And echoes of Turnbull's business style do reverberate in his approach to politics.

In the unblinking pursuit of Fairfax, for example, one can easily spot the seeds of Turnbull's hostile take-over of the seat of Wentworth. In both circumstances, he used a combination of lateral thinking, charm, brutality and astute legal manoeuvring to extract results.

Turnbull's entrée to the seat of Wentworth was not without bloodshed. No, that's a drab way of putting it; let's say that in order to contest the seat for the Liberal Party, Turnbull had first to remove a stubborn sitting member, Peter King, in circumstances of – for the Liberal Party – sickening political violence. In the course of this process, an estimated 1500 new members were signed up to Turnbull's home branch of Point Piper. Cynics call this "branch-stacking." Euphemists call it "growing democracy."

Turnbull's tactics were shockingly unorthodox, and sometimes ill-judged. For instance, he took out paid ads, in which Alan Jones read endorsements of him on air. This was unprecedented for an internal pre-selection process. Details of the Turnbull camp's branch-stacking efforts (they had signed 450 new members to the party's Point Piper branch) were leaked several weeks before the cutoff date for new members, ensuring an orgy of retribution.

The King forces stacked back just as fast as they could, and Turnbull countered with complicated legal challenges to the official status of their stackees.

King fought determinedly, but in the end was utterly outclassed. "When he came up against Turnbull, he came up against a speeding train," mused Alexander Downer. John Howard, who has in the past intervened to protect sitting members from this sort of attack, sat on his hands.

"I think I can put it this way," the former prime minister said, smiling broadly, when asked if he supported Turnbull's bid. "I didn't stop him getting pre-selection for Wentworth. He was prepared to have a go and I quite respected that. I didn't have anything against Peter King, but on the other hand Peter had knocked off the previous sitting member and I didn't think he could cry foul against Malcolm."

Before nominating for Wentworth, Turnbull sent a careful inquiry via the former party director Lynton Crosby to ascertain whether Howard would object to his candidacy. No such objection was expressed.

Much mythology built up, over the years, about the enmity between Malcolm Turnbull and John Howard. There was, of course, the business of

Turnbull's verbal attack on Howard at the end of his unsuccessful campaign for an Australian republic, in which he called Howard "the prime minister who broke the nation's heart."

But the recipient of that slap didn't take it much to heart. "Oh, I didn't care about *that*," he said when I asked him about it.

Howard could have stopped Turnbull getting pre-selection for Wentworth, and didn't. It was Howard who would give Turnbull his first big job in politics. It was Howard who would – many years later – counsel Turnbull to rethink his decision to quit federal politics after losing the Liberal leadership. And it was Howard who would bound forth to congratulate and endorse Turnbull in a press conference on the day he unseated Abbott, who reportedly was wounded by the haste of his old mentor's abandonment.

Turnbull's takeover of Wentworth had all the sweep and grandeur of a Labor branch-stack. When he arrived in Canberra, it was to a Coalition scandalised by the scale of the violence: it was as if a genteel bridge party had now to contend with a barbarian wearing the freshly flayed skin of the deputy secretary for scones.

Nor did much of the new environment naturally accord with Malcolm the Barbarian. He was flummoxed to learn that he would have to fill out, by hand, a declaration of all his assets and interests.

The Register of Members' Interests is a pleasantly anachronistic ritual, breach of which is nonetheless a catastrophic error. New and returning MPs are issued with photocopied forms, with spaces for things such as "real property" and "commercial investments." By picking up a completed set of forms and weighing it in one's hand, eyes closed, one can make a fair guess as to the political allegiance of the author. Labor MPs have, on the whole, shorter declarations, although earnest left-wingers wishing to make much of their modest circumstances will occasionally stray in the other direction by declaring everything from their Westpac Handycard account to the two bucks they gave to the Salvation Army collector on 15 January.

Liberal and National Party MPs are much more likely to have complicated share holdings, and family trusts called "Macbarhel" or "Sartombri" or some other clunky agglomerate of their children's names.

Malcolm Turnbull's declaration, however, was seriously weighty. Returning to parliament in 2007, Turnbull declared shareholdings in four listed companies, five unlisted public companies, eight private companies and twenty-five managed funds.

At the very end of the form is a space in which MPs are asked if there is anything at all remaining to declare; any asset worth more than $7500 after all the other categories have been covered. Most MPs have by now exhausted their worldly goods, but Turnbull had enough left for a brutally affluent final volley: "Boats, Artwork, Books, Furniture."

The gory dispatching of Peter King gave Turnbull senior ogre status in the parliamentary Liberal Party before he even got there.

"Some of them loathed him because of it," Downer says. "There's this sort of idea that particularly less-worthy backbenchers have that there is sort of a pecking order. They thought he was a *parvenu*."

The *Oxford English Dictionary* defines a *parvenu* as "A person from a humble background who has rapidly gained wealth or an influential social position; a *nouveau riche*; an upstart, a social climber."

"There was a bit of jealousy and bitterness about him," concludes Downer. "My advice to him was 'just go quietly, and you'll rise.'"

Another who offered Turnbull advice during this period, oddly enough given what was to come, was Brendan Nelson. Nelson says he approached Turnbull in the poky backbencher's office to which the former merchant banker was initially assigned.

"I said to him: 'Look – I don't ever forget being elected myself. You've achieved a lot in your life – far more than I have in mine. Sometimes you'll look at someone who is a minister and you'll think, 'Why is he a minister when I'm a backbencher? I'm much

smarter than him.' But the important thing is to realise that none of us is any better or any worse than
anybody else. There are people I work with here that
I don't like. But they'll never know that I don't like
them. You've got to rise from obscurity.'"

Nelson's little homily was sincere; he was
impressed by Turnbull's accomplishments, and genuinely concerned as to what Turnbull would make of
his new surroundings, littered as they were with people who were considerably stupider than Turnbull,
but considerably senior to him. Turnbull was keen to
prove himself a humble learner. But his famous attributes in law and business – impatience, and vaulting
ambition – were soon to assert themselves.

*

In late November 2007 the Liberal Party lost government, of course. It lost its leader, too, in an outcome
that was probably kindest for him; voted out of his
own seat, John Howard was not obliged to choose
between shrivelling away publicly on the back
benches or submitting the innocent people of Benne-
long to a by-election.

But then it lost its Plan B. Peter Costello, to the
amazement of nearly everyone, decided not to lead
the Liberals after all. At a press conference on the
Sunday after the election, he announced that he

would be leaving politics in due course to embark upon a career in the corporate world.

When Costello announced he would depart rather than take up the leadership, it was as though the backbone had been removed from the Liberal Party. Stripped of the two men who had given it form and substance for thirteen years, this luckless invertebrate flopped about in search of a new leader.

Malcolm Turnbull was quick to step up. So quick, in fact, that there are a couple of MPs and senators who reckon they only became aware of Peter Costello's withdrawal when Turnbull called them seeking their support. Nelson, after a lot of thought, decided to run too.

"I knew it was going to be hard, it was going to be thankless. I knew all that. But I believe in life you've got to have a go. I had a lot of support. And I'd seen a bit of Malcolm in the twelve months he'd been in cabinet. Enough to motivate me to see that there would be a contest."

There was a strange, light-headed feel about the short campaign that ensued before Coalition MPs and senators gathered in Canberra to make the choice between Nelson and Turnbull. For many, it was like one of those childhood dreams in which all the roles are played by the wrong people; where you turn up to school and you notice that you're not at school at all, but at the Easter Show, and your teacher's turned into Daryl Somers, and you're wearing a snorkel.

"The problem with that ballot is that nobody saw it coming," says Howard. "Nobody expected there to be a ballot between Brendan Nelson and Malcolm Turnbull."

Turnbull was convinced, with Costello out of the way, that he was the obvious choice. On the day before the leadership ballot, Turnbull gave an interview to Fran Kelly, of the ABC's Radio National. It was a confident performance; too confident for some.

KELLY: In the past, sometimes John Howard's leadership was described as mean and tricky. Would you describe yours, if you were Liberal leader, as more generous?

TURNBULL: Very much so.

KELLY: Should WorkChoices be dumped?

TURNBULL: Look, there is no question that Kevin Rudd has a mandate to make changes to WorkChoices.

KELLY: Would you support Labor in saying "Sorry" to the stolen generations?

TURNBULL: Unquestionably. That was, look, that was an error. I say this about, you know, a friend, John Howard: that was an error. Clearly, we should have said sorry then.

The above is an edited selection of Turnbull's remarks.

There was plenty about the interview that grated with Liberals who knew there had to be some renovations, but weren't quite prepared for the sight of Turnbull with his raised sledgehammer. To Turnbull's great surprise, Brendan Nelson won the ballot, with 45 votes to 42.

"That was a silly interview," is Howard's assessment of Turnbull's campaign style. "He probably did think he was going to win, and that damaged him. The issue that he floated in that interview – the apology – is an example of the danger that politicians get into. The apology had a huge run and everybody says Rudd did a good job with it ... but it didn't shift a vote."

The former PM has moved seamlessly into metapolitics here. He's not making a point about the merits of a national apology, in the argument over which his own position in government ended up hopelessly ensnarled in a brain-numbing semiotic debate about the difference between regret and remorse. He's making a point about the political smarts of Malcolm Turnbull for even raising it. (As for the apology itself: "I demonstrated my position by not attending. It would have been hypocritical for me to go.")

Nelson was overcome with emotion and humility upon his election to the leadership. Like a long-shot actor finding himself on stage grasping an Oscar, Nelson gave a teary speech in which he thanked Malcolm Turnbull, John Howard, Peter Costello, Mark Vaile and Alexander Downer, before solemnly warning his remaining colleagues that they faced a long and difficult road ahead.

Turnbull couldn't quite believe he had lost. "It was like the captain of the football team, who was also the rowing blue and the captain of the debating team and dux of the school, watching as the headmaster chooses someone else to be head boy," recalls one colleague. And he was disgusted by Nelson's weepy display. After the meeting but before Nelson's first press conference, Turnbull barrelled into Nelson's office, startling the small group that was already in there with the new leader.

"Brendan, that was terrible. It was funereal!" he stormed, waving his arms in the full Turnbull display. "Come on! You have to gee them up, like a football coach. Not depress them!"

Several weeks later, when Nelson was out in the car, Turnbull rang him again. "Let's face it, Brendan," he said. "You're just no good at this. The best thing you could do is just step down."

Recalling the intervention in Nelson's office, Turnbull grimaces. "I was trying to help him!" he protests.

In Turnbull's view, it was absolutely plain that Nelson was going to be a disaster. It was equally plain, in Turnbull's mind, that Turnbull would do a considerably better job. Giving Nelson tips on how to address their colleagues was, on that basis, a kindness rather than an assault.

*

The *Spycatcher* case, which fell into Turnbull's lap as a very young lawyer, was the perfect job for him – it involved deep legal detail, the chance to do his own thrilling gumshoe detective work, a stoutly defensible principle of freedom, and the possibility that he would shock the world.

Lucy Turnbull says that – in a funny way – *Spycatcher* ruined the law for her husband, as a lifelong career.

"Honestly, I think because the *Spycatcher* case was so exciting, after that he thought to himself 'Can it get more exciting than that? Have I done the most exciting thing already, in my twenties?'" she says. "He loves all that adventurous stuff."

Sometimes though, intrigue and adventure can go horribly wrong. Of the misfortunes that befell Malcolm Turnbull during his first stint in the Liberal leadership, easily the most exotically Turnbullesque was the Godwin Grech affair. On paper, it was a thrilling proposition. A mole inside the Treasury, feeding intelligence about the government's activities to a hungry Opposition. Tipoffs from Grech, a Treasury official with sympathies for the Liberal Party, allowed the Turnbull Opposition to keep one jump ahead of the Rudd government at several points during the global financial crisis of 2008. Turnbull demanded that the Australian Office of Financial Management should buy residential mortgage-backed securities; a week later, treasurer Wayne Swan announced that very measure. Turnbull proposed that the government should guarantee bank deposits to an unprecedented degree: voilà! So it came to pass.

But it was when Grech supplied the Opposition with purported details about the Rudd government's operation of a car financing assistance scheme – OzCar – that Turnbull saw the opportunity for something much, much bigger: the bringing down of a prime minister.

Grech had – he said – an email from a staffer in Rudd's office asking for special treatment for a Queensland car dealer. The dealer was a supporter of Rudd's and had given him a car for campaign purposes. At a secret meeting – staged, for clandestine purposes, in Lucy Turnbull's office – Turnbull was shown the email, as were Senate leader Eric Abetz and his chief of staff. A Treasury spy! A secret email! A whiff of corruption at the top! Prime ministerial blood in the water!

In parliament, Turnbull carefully laid the groundwork, seeking and obtaining from Rudd a denial that his office had in any way sought to influence the scheme's treatment of the dealer.

When Grech, appearing before a Senate committee inquiry, finally in public mentioned the existence of an email from Rudd's office, Turnbull was primed and ready to spring his trap. "These are grave allegations that reach the highest offices in the government of our nation," he declaimed in a portentous baritone, before a crush of transfixed journalists. "The prime minister and the treasurer have used their offices and taxpayers' resources to seek advantage for one of their mates and then lied about it to the parliament. If the prime minister and the treasurer cannot immediately justify their actions to the Australian people, they have no choice but to resign."

Tone is important in politics. By calling a press conference, by alleging that the prime minister was corrupt, by demanding his resignation, Turnbull elevated the OzCar matter to code-orange importance.

And when – unbelievably – it was revealed that the psychologically troubled Grech had in fact faked up the email in his own home, the altitude of Turnbull's allegations made the fall just that much more sickening.

The Grech affair wounded Turnbull horribly. The loss of credibility and face damaged him more broadly, as well as shaking his confidence, and by mid-2009 the public polls by which Canberra politicians set their heart rates had registered the most rapid drop in approval ratings for an Opposition leader in recorded history.

*

The end of Turnbull's brief term as Opposition leader is worth recalling in detail. Not only because it tells us a lot about his aims and methods, but also because the seven days over which he met his end is a wild, improbable but ultimately incredibly potent series of events in Australian political history.

Turnbull – as environment minister in the Howard government – had tried to cajole Howard into ratifying the Kyoto Protocol on climate change, and had successfully lobbied Howard to adopt a model of an emissions trading scheme. Turnbull's view was that there was strong public sympathy for doing something about climate change. Nelson's "wait for the world" approach as leader of the Opposition annoyed Turnbull, who felt that the Liberals' future as a modern party depended on a modern outlook on climate.

Soon after he took Nelson's place as leader, Turnbull and chief negotiator Andrew Robb, for the Coalition, sat down in August with the Rudd government, in the form of climate change minister Penny Wong, to arrive at an agreed model for an emissions trading scheme. In September, Robb took leave to seek treatment for a longstanding depressive illness, which had dogged him for much of his life. Robb was replaced by Queensland frontbencher Ian Macfarlane, who duly secured – with Wong – an agreed design for an emissions trading scheme, which Turnbull bustled through shadow cabinet and presented to his party room on the morning of 24 November.

The mood in that room was already fairly spicy. Climate sceptics, including Nick Minchin and Tony Abbott, were against the deal and had opposed it in shadow cabinet. Backbenchers – many confused by the monstrously complex deal – spoke for and against it at the meeting in roughly equal numbers.

But it was Andrew Robb who set off an incendiary chain of events. He had procured a copy of the agreement the day before and locked himself in his Canberra flat with it. Robb spent several hours studying the detail, and over that time came to the view that the proposal was a disaster.

Keep in mind: Turnbull assumed throughout that Robb would be a supporter. Robb didn't turn up for shadow cabinet and didn't mention to anyone his reservations about the ETS agreement. But he decided that it was his responsibility to blow the thing up, in the interests of his party and of the country. He showed up at the party-room meeting, and waited for his chance to speak.

Robb's account of this meeting, published in his memoir *Black Dog Daze*, reads like a John le Carré thriller. He recalls making an aside to Turnbull loyalist Michael Ronaldson, the Victorian Liberal senator, that the deal was "not all it's cracked up to be," then seeing Ronaldson pull Christopher Pyne out for a chat, after which Pyne re-entered the room and dropped a note in front of Turnbull, who was chairing the meeting.

As the meeting wore on, Robb became convinced that Pyne had tipped Turnbull off; every attempt Robb made to get his leader's attention was ignored. He worried that he would not be called upon to speak at all. Robb's perception was that the speakers – some for, some against – were simply repeating their existing views on climate change. None of them understood what the complex package actually meant.

"I ripped off a piece of paper – I didn't feel that good about doing this, but the stakes were high for our country – and wrote to Malcolm: 'The side effects of the medication I am on now make me very tired. I'd be really grateful if you could get me to my feet soon.'"

A few speakers later, Turnbull called on Robb, who got to his feet and unleashed a point-by-point critique of the deal's weaknesses. Having prevailed on Turnbull's sympathy for his illness, Robb repaid the kindness with a deadly evisceration of Turnbull's most-prized policy objective. His speech crystallised the nebulous fears of some in the room and undoubtedly swung the party's mood towards rejection of the deal. Some present recall tumultuous applause and a standing ovation.

The meeting now swerved out of Turnbull's control. The balance was tipped in favour of rejecting the proposal. But when senators left to attend a division, Turnbull – in their absence – counted the "yes" votes from the meeting, added those to the front-bench assents from earlier in the day, and declared the proposition carried by a slender margin. All merry hell broke loose. The meeting was suspended.

Turnbull was incandescent with rage. Robb – who had left the meeting soon after speaking – caught the full force of a Turnbull phone call in the break, replete with elaborately unflattering assessments of his character.

Robb is a man of gentle and vaguely ursine demeanour, but he too has worked for Kerry Packer. He's not easily intimidated.

"Malcolm can be ruthless; he just goes for broke, stares people down and walks over the top of them," he wrote. "He'll do anything to close a deal, and he's very effective at it. There's no doubt that if I'd given him any indication of the extent of my concerns, I would have been the last speaker or he would have had people lined up to diffuse the issues. But after I spoke, there were still six hours of debate left, as it turned out. Ian and Malcolm had every opportunity to address the concerns I presented; they didn't, which said it all."

The meeting was on Tuesday, 25 November. On Wednesday, Kevin Andrews called for a spill of Turnbull's leadership. The motion was defeated 48–35, an uncomfortably close result. On Thursday, senior right-wingers Nick Minchin and Tony Abbott visited Turnbull, told him they couldn't support his deal, and resigned their front-bench positions.

On Friday, Scott Morrison – the man who, as state director of the Liberal Party, popped into Turnbull's

Goldman Sachs office in 2000 to deliver a member-ship form so that the banker could rejoin the Liberal Party – visited to tell him that he had to let go of the carbon policy. "Let it go, or this is it," he told the Opposition leader. "It's all over." Turnbull did not take it well. The two men – friends, off and on – would not speak again for years.

On Sunday, Turnbull strapped explosives all over himself, telling Laurie Oakes in a breakfast television interview that if Minchin and fellow sceptics got their way, "we will end up becoming a fringe party of the far right." He told Oakes that he had been assured, just hours earlier, by aspiring leader Joe Hockey that Hockey too believed the carbon deal should be passed.

Oddly enough, Monday found most of the inter-ested parties in the Liberal leadership – bar the man who still held it – shuffling in and out of meetings in Joe Hockey's office.

Hockey – convinced Turnbull was not going to be a candidate if the spill motion was passed, signifying a loss of faith in him – had decided over the weekend to stand for the leadership. He still supported the ETS deal, and was not prepared to renounce it to win sup-port from the Right.

Weirdly, though, Monday found him caucusing with just about everybody else – including the most assiduous opponents of the deal. Leadership challenges do not usually work like this. Julie Bishop, still Malcolm Turnbull's deputy, was invited to participate. "Um, you know I need to tell Malcolm about this? I'm the deputy leader," she pointed out.

Off she went to tell Turnbull. "I've been invited to a meeting in Joe Hockey's office," she announced.

"Hmm? Okay." He seemed distracted.

At the meeting, all sorts of arrangements were canvassed. Nick Minchin, party director Brian Loughnane, George Brandis, Peter Dutton, Andrew Robb, Tony Abbott – all passed through Hockey's office over the course of the day.

"Dutton's going to run as deputy," Hockey declared at one point. This came as a surprise to the serving deputy, Julie Bishop, who had not realised her job was up for grabs.

Hockey, as a less-abrasive version of Turnbull, was thought the most likely successor. In a straight vote, he would be thought a more rational selection than Tony Abbott, who for most of Monday was not a declared candidate. But would it be a straight vote? Hockey thought he had a commitment from Turnbull that he wouldn't run. Julie Bishop walked back to her office after one of these meetings broke up, accompanied by Tony Abbott.

"If I ran for the leadership and I won, I'd be very happy for you to remain as my deputy," he said.

"Well, the others are going to split," said Bishop. "Everyone can see that except Joe. Malcolm's going to run."

Later that night, Abbott announced that he would be a candidate. Joe Hockey announced that if he were to become leader, he would allow a conscience vote on the climate deal. Both of these factors went into the cauldron. When Liberal MPs met the next morning, the popular expectation was that Joe Hockey would be the next leader of the Liberal Party. It was an expectation shared by respondents to Newspoll, of whose respondents 33 per cent chose Hockey, 30 per cent Turnbull and 19 per cent Abbott.

What happened next was one of those vertiginous series of events that remind us that politics – despite our assumptions to the contrary – is sometimes not governed by rules or process or rational assumption. Sometimes it is governed by a freakish mixture of personality quirk and cosmic accident.

And so, when the Liberal Party met on the morning of 24 November, and the motion to spill the leadership was passed 48–34 – a clear expression of no confidence in Malcolm Turnbull – the contest did not become, as Joe Hockey and many others were expecting, one between Joe Hockey and Tony Abbott.

When candidates for the leadership were called, Malcolm Turnbull stood up. There were gasps. And instant confusion. In the first vote, Turnbull got 26 votes. Abbott 35. And Hockey only 23, which eliminated him from the process, meaning the final vote was between Abbott and Turnbull.

And it was that vote – that matter of minutes, as eighty-four grown adults scribbled furiously on small pieces of paper, folding them solemnly and sticking them in a box only to be drawn out again, with great ceremony, and counted – that proved a mighty fulcrum in the affairs of the Liberal Party, and indeed the country.

Tony Abbott won by one vote, collecting forty-two to Turnbull's forty-one. There was one ballot that was spoiled, its author simply scrawling "No."

The assumption that most people make about politics is that it is governed by rules. It's an easy mistake to make; the semblance of regulation is everywhere, from the archaic standing orders of parliament to the rules of the Caucus and Coalition party rooms, to the cramped social etiquette of the public service. But the juice in the machine is anarchically human; the largest decisions of our age can and are made on the diciest of premises.

Is it possible, for instance, that if Robb had not faked some symptoms that day, and had indeed not been called upon to speak until late in the piece, that a relevant number of Coalition MPs might have remained confused about the import of the ETS package, and voted for it anyway out of politeness or sense of duty?

If Turnbull hadn't already been so damaged by the Grech affair, in which his lifelong lucky streak failed him monstrously, would he have been so brittle with his party on the issue of the emissions trading scheme?

"It's like he had a death wish," recalls one colleague. "He didn't think he would get the deal. He wanted martyrdom, and to be defeated on principle rather than incompetence."

That week in politics changed everything. The Robb intervention spelled the end of Turnbull. The end of Turnbull itself was a finely balanced affair that propelled Tony Abbott into the leadership by the narrowest of margins. Which was a surprise to him, and to the party, and to Kevin Rudd, whose first thought was that all his Christmases had come at once. Rudd soon discovered, however, that in the loss of the climate legislation, and its subsequent shelving, there existed the seeds of his own destruction. And from Rudd's destruction, brought about brutally and with scant notice by the woman who had been his deputy since the beginning, there sprouted the retributive animosity that in time would bring her down too.

Australian politics set off, that night in 2009, on a path of multilateral vengeance and suspicion that would last six years. It's not even finished yet, necessarily. But never again would the two great Australian parties attempt a grand bargain on anything so contentious as climate change. They learnt to keep apart, because on both sides the penalties of consensus had proven too steep.

Seven years after Malcolm Turnbull's handshake deal with Labor, he is fighting – as prime minister this time – a federal election campaign in which he is explicitly opposing carbon-pricing principles he once endorsed at much personal cost. Indeed, in the years after 2009, as first Julia Gillard and then Kevin Rudd walked the Labor Party's policy on asylum seekers back towards the Howard government's model they had once decried, the two parties never formally acknowledged that they now agreed with each other on that policy too.

From being close enough to shake hands, as the two parties were for those precious few weeks in 2009, they blew apart with an exothermic force, and would never intentionally touch again.

*

His failure as leader of the Liberal Party was a terrible blow for Turnbull. Lucy whisked him away soon after for a long overseas trip and the pair of them forgot about politics for a while.

"Lucy decided ... that the best thing to do would be to get me away on a holiday and, just, get me out of it because it was a very tough year, and losing a position like that is an enormous blow, a very big blow, even if it is, you know, anticipated," he said. "It's a very, very big blow, and maintaining an equitable state of mind is not easy, and Lucy was a very smart person and she recognised that, ah, this was a time when intensive husband maintenance was top of the priority list."

When parliament resumed in February 2010, however, the reality kicked in.

"Well, it was a very bleak period, Annabel, there is no point, you know ... I'm not kidding, I'm not being self-pitying or anything like that, but it was a very, very tough period, a very bleak period," Turnbull recalled.

"I thought about should I stay in parliament and I announced that I wasn't going to run again and, then I was, you know rather overwhelmed and humbled by all the people that said no, no you must stay and so then I changed my mind [*laughs*] and fortunately the electors of Wentworth forgave me, and re-elected me. But it was a ... it's a rough business. Politics is a very very rough business."

Turnbull announced he would quit politics in April 2010. But he was quickly overtaken by agonising doubt.

"I think it became pretty clear after he made the decision that he hadn't made the right one," recalls Lucy. "That was a difficult time. Most of the time, once you've made a decision, you think 'Phew.' But from the time that decision was made it was pretty clear that he regretted it."

John Howard, Arthur Sinodinos and pollster Mark Textor were among those who counselled Turnbull to change his mind and stay on as the Member for Wentworth. Which he did, winning the seat in 2010.

And when Tony Abbott won the 2013 election and was sworn in as prime minister, he made Malcolm Turnbull the minister for communications.

A close friend says that something changed in Turnbull after the loss of the leadership. "That ambition that had driven him just moderated a bit. I think the pain of the whole experience was so great that he came to the – it's difficult, because he doesn't analyse himself all that much – but I think he came to the conclusion that he wouldn't invest so much in it again. I genuinely think he decided, in 2010, that if the highest he rose again would be as a Coalition cabinet minister, he would be okay with that."

A couple of postscripts: Turnbull reconciled with

Scott Morrison a few months out from the 2013 election. Morrison invited him to go kayaking on the Hacking River in his electorate. Equably, the two men paddled along, through gorges flanked by supplejack, Bangalow palm and golden sassafras, chatting about this and that, burying the hatchet.

In time, Turnbull forgave even Andrew Robb. Robb, who overcame his problems with depression and went on as trade minister to become one of the few unalloyed successes of the Abbott government, made a couple of overtures to Turnbull in 2010, then kept his distance. But in 2012 things defrosted. En route to the same function, Turnbull invited Robb up to his Canberra apartment for dinner and a glass of wine.

"I told him it was nothing personal," recalls Robb. "He said something accepting of that. There are lots of haters in politics. I'm not one of them, and I don't think he is either."

"This is one of the big things John Howard taught me," says Robb. "After we won the 1996 election, he put Wilson Tuckey into the cabinet, and he put John Moore into the ministry. These are the guys who most publicly talked, in a demeaning way, about how they'd finished him off as leader the last time. I said, 'How come you've got them where you've got them?' And Howard said: 'Andrew, in this business you've got to forgive. But you never forget.'"

Pants Off

When he was Liberal leader the first time around, Malcolm Turnbull's temper was a variable as widely discussed as the weather. Colleagues swapped stories of being snapped at or frozen out. Turnbull's own staff – acutely aware of their boss's capacity to shift from ebullience to gloom to anger – developed their own triage system to assess his moods.

It was known, around the office, as the "Pants Off" scale. The expression originated with an especially fruity eruption of the Turnbull temper early one morning in March 2009, when – ensconced in an Adelaide hotel – the Liberal leader greeted a member of staff at the door to his room wearing a business shirt and boxer shorts, and bellowing with frustration about the shortcomings of his office.

Turnbull – himself a gifted writer – periodically expressed frustration with the standard of speeches and articles compiled by his staff. On this occasion, he had been offered a slot in the pages of the *Australian* to respond to an essay Kevin Rudd had published in the *Monthly*, arguing that capitalism was broken, and that it now fell to Rudd and other social democrats to save capitalism from itself. It is difficult to overstate how risible Turnbull found this idea.

The copy for the *Australian* was due late morning. Turnbull had been out to dinner the night before with John Howard and Alexander Downer, and on coming home, had reviewed the version his staff had put together; unhappy, he had worked on it until late, and daybreak found him in a foul mood.

"If I had any f--king staff who were any good, I might have a chance!" he ranted – pantless – at the surprised staffer, as hotel staff wheeled breakfast trolleys discreetly by. "Why do I have to do all this stuff myself?"

The incident, for the final six months of Turnbull's time as Opposition leader, assumed benchmark status. Staff would exchange intelligence as to his mood before attempting important interactions. "Pants Off" denoted serious anger, while "Half Pants Off" merely signified extreme tetchiness. Sometimes, during a phone hook-up, staff would exchange glances and mime the unzipping of their trousers as Turnbull's disembodied voice grew angrier in tone.

(Surely it is not unforgivably sentimental to pause at this point to consider a quaint historical symmetry in

Australian politics. This nation has had two Liberal prime ministers called Malcolm. The first – Malcolm Fraser – became notorious after leaving office for turning up in a Memphis hotel without his trousers. And the second Malcolm will live on – in the minds of a small but influential group of people – as a stressed-out man in an Adelaide hotel room, dressed impeccably from the waist up.)

Now: one of the first things to say about Malcolm Turnbull's second stint in the leadership of the Liberal Party is that his pants have remained – so far – largely in place. Where once the air was thick with tales of Turnbull rages, or the acidly fluent character assessments for which he has been famous his whole life, the early part of his prime ministership has been reasonably calm on that front.

"That's what happens when you get what you want," observes one cabinet colleague shortly.

Of the staff who joked about "Pants Off," quite a few have returned to work in the prime minister's office. One points out, in retrospect (and with a note of remorse about the trouser meme): "It was a very difficult time. Opposition is hard. To take the hardest and most thankless job in the parliament – Opposition leader – with only four years' parliamentary experience, is very stressful."

Turnbull is seven years older now than he was

when he first led the Liberal Party. That's seven years' more political experience. Now, he is the oldest person in the cabinet, and one of only two in that group – Julie Bishop is the other – who sat in the cabinet of John Howard.

John Howard himself had a not-very-successful initial stint in the Liberal leadership, as leader of the Opposition. He lost the job to Andrew Peacock in 1989, and did not regain it until 1995; six years of humiliation and reflection, during which time his reign as Australia's most successful contemporary Liberal prime minister was all but unimaginable.

Turnbull's time in the wilderness was weirdly similar: six years, from his dumping in November 2009 until his resurrection in 2015.

Howard – when he lost the leadership in 1989 – commented curtly that the prospect of his regaining the job lived in "Lazarus with a triple bypass" territory.

Twenty years later, Malcolm Turnbull not only was rejected by his colleagues, but also burned the villages on his way out. Lazarus with a triple bypass, two black eyes and a serious hamstring injury.

Howard, too, in his chaotic first term in government, was accused of directionlessness and panic, for all that he is now recalled as a beacon of calm. His masterly 1996 landslide victory over Paul Keating – which produced a horde of blinking Coalition newcomers in

Canberra – all but entirely receded in 1998, an election in which Kim Beazley won more than 50 per cent of the vote nationally for Labor, and went consternatingly close to winning.

Most people around Malcolm Turnbull – the closest enthusiastically, the farthest far more grudgingly – will tell you that Malcolm Mark II is an improvement on Malcolm Mark I.

"There's a significant contrast," says deputy leader and foreign minister Julie Bishop. "The current Malcolm is very self-assured, very zen, very good-humoured. Nothing fazes him. He's not panicked by anything that goes on. He's immune to the media criticisms; he knows what he wants and in his mind he knows where he's going."

"Since he became leader, he's been as relaxed and comfortable as he's ever been," says a longtime friend. "He doesn't care about the accoutrements of state – the fancy cars, the people bowing in front of him. It's that he's got the job and he's able to do things."

Malcolm Turnbull's decision-making process hasn't changed all that much since that awful summer when he learnt about the water on his dad's farm. When a project interests him, he pitches himself in head-first. He is the kid who takes apart the motorbike and learns how to put it back together. He has to have all the information; all the briefings.

"He's a deal guy," says one close witness to Turnbull's method in office. "He gets every element of information before he makes a decision. Most politicians look for the information that confirms what they want to do. But what he's doing is making sure he hasn't missed anything."

It's not a typical approach for a political leader. It's more reminiscent of a barrister, building a case, who wants to establish where the weak points lie. Or a merchant banker, doing due diligence on a big deal. Or a CEO, sweeping the area looking for good ideas and clever people. Turnbull has been all of those things.

"I know what he's doing!" says one cabinet colleague. "It's how he's been successful at life in general. He has all these fabulous people around to dinner parties and he picks their brains, then invests in something that everyone else thinks is a lemon and then it turns out to be a smash hit."

And it remains true that the dream political manoeuvre for Malcolm Turnbull is one that incorporates efficiency, elegance, originality and surprise. For these reasons, Turnbull likes to have every available option open, for as long as possible. He likes to hear all arguments, and will be as engaged by the arguments against a proposition as he is by the arguments for.

I ring George Brandis. He is also a barrister, and one of the cabinet members who might occasionally

challenge Turnbull's automatic claim to "smartest person in the room" status. I ask him whether Turnbull's
"Socratic dialogue approach" to decision-making is
unusual for politics.

There is a pause.

"I'm not sure 'Socratic dialogue' is really quite
right," he muses. "It's more of an Aristotelian sym-
posium approach than a Socratic approach."

Unsure of my next move, I opt for silence.

"He's a very democratic leader," says Brandis,
eventually. "Malcolm consciously sees himself as
relying on his cabinet colleagues to be his counsel-
lors. There's less of a sense of the PMO [prime
minister's office] being a hermit kingdom."

The term "hermit kingdom" (as I self-loathingly
ascertain from Wikipedia five seconds after hanging up
the phone) is one applied to "any country, organisation
or society which willfully walls itself off, either meta-
phorically or physically, from the rest of the world."
Usually, it's a term identified with North Korea.

Not everyone's a fan of the Aristotelian sympo-
sium. One critic – a Liberal insider – says the real
explanation is that Turnbull is just disinclined to
make decisions. "In business, the more people you
talk to the better. But in politics, talking to more people doesn't necessarily get you a better decision. It
might get you a few alternatives that all look plausible

and doable and you can afford them, but the final decision is a judgment call. That's politics. And I'm not sure Malcolm is actually a politician."

While he was communications minister in the Abbott government, Turnbull was genuinely upset by the degree to which, he believed, the role of cabinet as the government's premier decision-making body was being subsumed by the two-person sub-committee of Tony Abbott and his chief of staff, Peta Credlin. Credlin attended cabinet meetings for the first year of the Abbott government; after the "near death experience" of his party's uprising in February 2015, Abbott conducted them without her, in deference to his colleagues' protests.

"Meetings actually got shorter after that," says one cabinet source. "Ministers thought, instinctively, well, what's the point of having long arguments in the cabinet, because Abbott will never make a decision without Credlin there. You'd just leave it till after the meeting, and go and see Credlin directly. The good thing about cabinet now is that the people who make the decisions are in the room."

The strongest lessons politicians learn are from the mistakes they have personally made in the past. The second strongest are from mistakes they watch others making. And Malcolm Turnbull learnt from the misadventure of his first period in the Liberal leadership that he needed to be more consultative.

"Last time around he was a complete and utter car crash," says another minister. "This time the essence of Malcolm is still there – the deal-maker. But he's very consciously listening to others."

This sounds – so far – eminently sensible. Who could possibly be against evidence? And reasoned discussion? And learning from mistakes?

But the "let's start at the beginning" approach to decision-making – especially on the big stuff – can create some procedural banana skins.

The prime minister, anxious to change the tone of political debate in this country, announced early in his term that the government would be taking a from-first-principles look at taxation. Treasury's existing review, which specifically excluded consideration of the GST, was sidelined in favour of a new and broader approach, which would consider all options. It would be a proper review, he said, with no foolish and premature rulings-out owing to political panic about potentially unpopular measures.

Everyone had a view. Treasurer Scott Morrison favoured a "tax-mix switch" – essentially an increase to the GST, offset by income-tax cuts.

Treasury itself, headed by Abbott-era appointment John Fraser, favoured a company-tax cut to increase productivity. But the process was overseen by Martin Parkinson, the former Treasury secretary.

Parkinson had been hustled out of the job by Tony Abbott, who fancied him as too left-wing, too sympathetic to Labor and too activist on climate change. Parkinson – reinstated resplendently by Turnbull last year to head the Department of Prime Minister and Cabinet – is on record extensively as supporting a shift towards indirect taxes like the GST.

The Business Council of Australia, in its submission, advocated an increase in the GST to fund a company-tax cut (a suggestion Turnbull described privately, according to the *Australian Financial Review*'s Laura Tingle, as the "go into the study, get out the service revolver and blow your brains out" option).

So many opinions. So much discussion. And with Turnbull engaging warmly with all protagonists, people walked away with different ideas about what his inclinations were.

"He will listen to the cons of a proposal with as much genuine interest and enthusiasm as the pros," says one intimate. "Some people find this confusing."

Morrison is accustomed to swift decision-making. His special skill is taking a tough proposition and defending it stoutly. In his former and most controversial job, as immigration minister, he maintained an attitude of granite-hard hostility to boat arrivals, fostering a close relationship with sympathetic newspapers and influential radio presenters to fulfil

Tony Abbott's promise to "stop the boats."

Morrison, in the first few months of the Turnbull government, was keen to get cracking. His impression from discussions with Turnbull was that Turnbull shared his preference for increasing the GST and using the proceeds to cut income taxes: the "tax-mix switch" option. As Christmas gave way to January and Turnbull kept talking to people, Morrison became worried that there would be insufficient time to prepare Australians for such a big change. In interviews, he sharpened his defence of a GST increase.

But the decision wasn't done and dusted. Backbench fury at the prospect of selling a tax increase, combined with modelling that showed only a moderate boost to economic growth, put Turnbull off the idea and he scotched it publicly.

It was an embarrassment for Morrison, who had booked a February appearance at the National Press Club to campaign on the idea, and in the end was obliged instead to deliver a low-key sermon on living within our means.

There are two streams of thought in the government on all this. One defends Turnbull. "Malcolm's view on tax reform was that everything was on the table," says a cabinet minister. "What he didn't factor in was the propensity of people to leak those discussions to the press. There will always be a public servant, no matter how junior, or a colleague, no matter how senior, who can't keep their flapping traps shut."

"In a naive way, he thought we should really have this discussion – have it internally, and then emerge with a clear policy. I think he has been quite shocked to find that you really can't do that."

Another cabinet colleague is more brutal, sheeting home the blame to Morrison for jumping the gun and creating the expectation of a GST increase well before there was any such decision from the government or Turnbull. "Scott is yet to learn that he can't be a tabloid player in this job like he was in border protection," says the colleague. "He wants to till the soil, to prepare people, but you can't till the soil before the decision is made. Now he's the treasurer, his words are bullets."

"I just think Scott didn't read Malcolm properly," says one senior bureaucrat with eyes on the evolving situation.

Turnbull himself told Melbourne radio interviewer Neil Mitchell on 22 March 2016: "I am a different prime minister to some of my predecessors. I believe that government should look at these issues very carefully, take all of the issues, matters into account, confer confidentially in the cabinet, and then, when we make a decision, announce it, rather than providing hints and leaks and briefs and front-running."

The latter part of the remark was interpreted widely as a slap to Morrison.

In the intriguing case of Who Killed Tax Reform?, however, Scott Morrison is not without defenders, and they argue that Turnbull changes his mind. That he can commit to one course of direction, then revise his view after talking to a new person who has swayed him. Sometimes without telling the witnesses to the first decision. There's something called the "Five Metre Rule." As in, are there more than five metres between the point at which an agreement is reached and the microphone at which Turnbull is scheduled to announce it? If there are, and somebody gets in his ear on the walk, you're in trouble.

In the end, what was revealed in the 2016 Budget was a compromise far more modest in scope than either man had originally intended: a ten-year plan for cutting company tax to 25 per cent, funded by raids on multi-national tax minimisers, the superannuation accounts of the very wealthy and the long-suffering Aussie smoker. The "soak the rich" connotations of the document chilled the enjoyment, in some Liberal hearts, of the support for small business. It did not go unnoticed that both the superannuation reforms and the cigarette excise increase were existing Labor policy.

Tensions between treasurers and prime ministers are a common and sometimes even productive feature

of government. They usually spring from professional rivalry (the treasurer wants the PM's job), from
conflicting objectives (the PM wants to buy the love
of the electorate with expensive baubles, the treasurer
would rather have a surplus) or from genuine ideological differences.

Is it possible that what we witnessed in the first six
months of the Turnbull government was that dullest
of all conflicts: a mismatch in political method?

There is no evidence – yet – of a poisonous personal
relationship between Turnbull and Morrison. They are
like two people in a conversation who stop and start and
accidentally talk over each other. The rhythm isn't there.
But neither has stopped hoping that it will happen.

The mismatch between Turnbull, whose roots are
in business, and Morrison – who has the mind of a
campaign director – also hints at a broader possibility, lent weight by Turnbull's fondness for ignoring
political orthodoxy.

Is there a chance that he just isn't that into politics? I mean: obviously he is *interested* in politics. But
he never seems very attracted to the elements of the
political process that are grim, grinding and almost
always, in the long term, associated with political success: constant repetition of a simple message; the
petty administrative brutality of shutting down dis-
sent on one's own side and cauterising potential

outlets for disunity. His office – full of clever people whom Turnbull has collected from various walks of life – is not a command and control centre.

The COAG misadventure drew for the first time – and this is chilling for any contemporary government – comparisons with the Rudd government. Big ideas, poorly thought-out and executed, then abandoned within days. A prime ministerial office working – at short notice – on a flurry of proposals that political orthodoxy would dictate should be developed over years, not months. Turnbull's enthusiasm for trains and his determination to bring a national approach to the planning of cities, for example, prompted a new interest in fast-train projects; these are the Moby Dicks of federal transport policy, totemic in spirit but awfully hard to get in the boat. Reports from several state premiers' offices dealing with the prime minister's office suggest that the overall impression is of chaos.

To some extent, this is to be expected. All new governments are hopeless at least for a bit, and in comparison with all the new governments this country has experienced in the last decade, the Turnbull government could in no way be classified as the worst. But a long campaign off a short runway has dangers all its own. And even for Malcolm Turnbull – a man who has always believed there is no orthodoxy alive incapable of subversion, to some degree, by his own potent combination of brilliance and charm – the capacity for horrendous misadventure under these circumstances is high.

The Optimist

Malcolm Turnbull is motivated by many things: curiosity, a delight in detail, a deep love of elegant solutions. A genuine sense of public service. What doesn't motivate him, especially, is ideology, beyond the basics that make him instinctively a liberal – a strong commitment to personal freedom and the virtues of a free market.

"Pragmatism, experience and commonsense will be better guides than ideology," he told the House of Representatives in his 2004 maiden speech.

"I am not an ideological person," he told Fran Kelly in 2007, on the occasion of his first run (unsuccessful) at the leadership of the Liberal Party. "I am a practical person. I come with a long experience in business. My interest is in things that work, in things that deliver real results for people that are relevant. I'm not interested in ideological wars."

"He's a problem-solver, not an ideologue," says George Brandis.

The term "ideologue" is not an attractive one. It is

easy to make the case, in theory, for a leader who is not bound by an ideological straitjacket.

But it's difficult for many in the Liberal Party, who would prefer there to be some sort of jacket involved. And the fact that the most successful Liberal prime minister in living memory – John Howard – was much more forcibly driven by ideology doesn't help.

"Ideology has to drive policy decisions – shape them," says one deeply frustrated senior Coalition adviser. "How is it that we have a Coalition government that for three months now has been tossing around ideas about how to increase tax? We're supposed to be about cutting tax!"

It's true that much of modern politics – particularly in the frenzied contemporary news cycle – is about tactics. But to attain that which makes life worth living, as Nietzsche wrote, is a "long obedience in the same direction."

Where does Turnbull's long obedience lead? Six years ago, I asked dozens of Turnbull's colleagues how Australia would be different if he were prime minister. What were his most closely held policy convictions? I asked them each to name three.

"You'll have to excuse me. I'm eating some chocolate," was the best initial response, from a Liberal on the other end of a phone line.

But most made, as their first answer, mention in some way or other of the word "freedom." Chief among these was Turnbull himself: "I believe passionately in a free society, in government enabling people to do their best rather than telling them what's best. It's really a question of making sure that people have the maximum choice, that we have as much competition as possible and that we eliminate obstacles to starting a business and managing a business."

To this central tenet, Turnbull added some specific policy interests, saying, "When I am prime minister, we will return to one of my policy fascinations, which is water and water management." He also said he wanted Australia to repair its spotty record on innovation, describing the country's relative dearth of intellectual-property-based industries as "one of our greatest failures, for a highly educated country. We've got to reward innovation more. Because the difficulty now is that people with innovative skills just go somewhere else." Lastly, he mentioned tax reform.

John Howard's assessment of Turnbull's central policy convictions was as follows:

He does believe in market-centred economics. He does believe in as small a role for government as is appropriate given the circumstances – I think he is quite genuine about that. And he does have a real understanding about the financial system. There aren't too many people who really understand it, and he's one of them. Peter Costello did, and I did, and I can't think of too many others. He is a stronger believer, he rests more … I think he genuinely does buy the scientific arguments about the climate, more so than I did. His instincts in what one might call family issues I think are quite conservative. He's sort of quite a family-man type person. Our views on things like gay marriage are not that different, and he had an atypical electorate. He empathised with the gay community, which is fine. They are the three things that have always hit me.

"Malcolm is an optimist," said Brandis. "As he often says, he's in the Liberal Party because he thinks it's all about encouraging people to be the best they can be, not telling them what to be. One of the things I find striking about Malcolm is that he is essentially not a cynical person."

Malcolm Turnbull's greatest moments in his career before politics were as an advocate: a champion with a brief. Given a case to defend, be it Kerry Packer's innocence of the "Goanna" allegations before the Costigan royal commission, or Peter Wright's book *Spycatcher*, he was a giant-killer. Packer, with whom

Turnbull had a relationship of intimate volatility, used him best of all. He directed Turnbull into negotiations where the young man's aggressiveness, and single-mindedness in pursuit of an outcome, were used to devastating effect. John Howard did something similar, in unleashing Turnbull on the rotten clubhouse of vested interests that was water management in Australia. In circumstances – like the republic referendum, or in leading his own party towards a particular climate policy in 2009 – where he is required to chart a direction for others to follow, Turnbull's results have been poorer.

As Opposition leader, Turnbull was a lawyer and a deal-maker, much as he had always been. As prime minister, he has cut his cloak according to his party's cloth. Conscious of his first and most important lesson from his first stint in leadership – that he must not foist his views too violently on his colleagues, or at least not right away – he has held the Abbott line even on issues upon which he fundamentally disagrees with the former leader. The party, now, is his most immediate and demanding client.

"He has a lawyer's intellect," one former employee told me. "I have never seen anybody able to absorb information in the way that he does. But you never hear him talking about what the conceptual, thematic link is."

Paul Keating, that savage verbal caricaturist, once said: "I fancy Malcolm is like the big red bunger. You light him up, there's a bit of a fizz, then nothing. Nothing."

Turnbull has professed himself to be unafraid of failure; that's a new one for prime ministers. When launching his innovation package at the CSIRO early in his term, Turnbull announced a tax incentive for risk-taking start-up companies.

When asked by a reporter whether there was a possibility such schemes could be rorted, Turnbull replied sunnily:

There are risks for everybody. And we've got to be prepared to take risks. That is why one of the aspects of the political paradigm I'm seeking to change is the old politics where politicians felt that they had to guarantee that every policy would work, they had to sort of water everything down so there was no element of risk. Let me tell you: I'm not guaranteeing that all of these policies will be as successful as we hope they will be. Actually, I'm very confident about it because we've worked very hard on it. We had a great team, we've had a lot of good collaboration, but, you know, if some of these policies are not as successful as we'd like, we will change them. And we will learn from them. Because that is what a twenty-first century government has got to be. It has got to be as agile as the start-up businesses it seeks to inspire.

There was an intake of breath as the reporters gathered the import of what this new prime minister was saying, which was, in effect: I hope these policies will work. They may not, of course! In which case we will try something else.

This is something you expect to hear from a highly evolved CEO or a venture capitalist. But you don't hear it from political leaders, who are trained quite hard to fear both failure and back-flips.

One supporter says that this frankness is the most refreshing thing about Turnbull. "It's very hard for the press gallery and the public to deal with someone who's being as honest as that," he says. "They're all used to the certainty of the Spartan regime, where Sparta is always right, and Athens must be destroyed."

*

In his influential 1973 essay "A Leader and a Philosophy," David Kemp (at that stage of his career, a very future Coalition minister) mounted a provocative argument about leadership.

"The first and most important relationship is between leader and followers, not between leader and the public," he wrote. Kemp was writing in January 1973, a month after Gough Whitlam bulldozed his way through the shambolic ranks of Billy McMahon's Liberal government in the "It's Time" election. The article – which paved the way for the ascent of Kemp's mentor, Malcolm Fraser, to the leadership – argued that too much had been made, in the past, of image and fuzzy notions of electoral appeal in the business of selecting Liberal leaders.

"Seeing leadership in terms of 'image' misses its most important ingredient," Kemp wrote. "The leader's first task is – as the very word implies – to *lead* the party he leads. The ultimate support of a leader's authority is his role as expounder of a philosophy or ideology which commands common consent and adherence in the party."

In Kemp's model, the existence of a philosophy itself is the crucial thing, regardless of its detail or tint.

For Turnbull, the establishment of a stable relationship with his followers in the party has clearly been his first order of business. When he challenged Tony Abbott for the leadership in September 2015, he committed none of the strategic internal clangers of which he had been guilty in the past. He did not burst into the media with complaints about the incumbent or telegraph his intentions privately with colleagues. He did not give lavish interviews outlining how he would change the party's direction. He kept his plans tight, and when he challenged Abbott, he did it first in person.

As prime minister, he has placed the reassurance of colleagues ahead of just about everything else – including the fulfilment of hopes in the electorate that he would immediately reverse Tony Abbott's entire legacy. Instead, he has placated the conservative wing of his party wherever possible. Retained the bulk of the climate policies of his predecessor. Kept Tony Abbott's schedule for a plebiscite on same-sex marriage. Taken the pinking shears to a schools' anti-bullying program that contained sympathetic material on transgender and same-sex-attracted teenagers.

Clearly, he would like to govern for some time, with the support of a still-conservative party that sleeps soundly at night safe in the knowledge it won't wake up unilaterally gay-married. The million-dollar question is: how long does this placatory approach last?

"He wants to get his own mandate," says one minister. "Once he gets his own mandate from the party, that will secure his position. Our party is still bruised from the spill, but once he gets his own mandate, he will be more secure in his position, and he will feel more secure in his position."

This is a popular view among his senior supporters. "When he gets his own mandate, as I believe he will, he will then be in a much stronger position," says another minister.

But secure his position to do what? If Malcolm Turnbull wins an election largely shrouded in the garb of his predecessor, then does that provide a mandate to do anything beyond more of the same?

Of all the lessons learnt from the magic prime-ministerial roundabout of the past ten years, surely the most lancing – the most arresting, by far – is that to say one thing before an election, and another after it, is an extremely bad idea.

Unpredictable prime ministerial behaviour is punished with astonishing consistency.

John Howard, who surprised voters with the industrial extremes of WorkChoices, paid the price in 2007.

Kevin Rudd's surprise was hitting the reverse-thrusters on climate policy, a challenge he had described as a towering and moral one. Also the mining tax.

Julia Gillard's surprise was the carbon tax. Tony Abbott's was that the budget repair enterprise, a job he had quoted as Opposition leader with a nod and a wink and a reassurance that it wouldn't hurt too much, turned out – in the 2014 budget – to be both more painful and more expensive than advertised. Australian voters responded as they would to any shonky tradesperson.

Malcolm Turnbull's exquisite dilemma is that to maintain peace in his own party he needs not to surprise his own colleagues before the 2016 election. But to change course after that event would be to commit the decade's most cardinal political sin.

The cause of all this tension is a peculiarly Liberal story. Stripping away all the eye-catching ephemera of the personalities involved, what happened to the Liberal Party in September 2015?

Two things. One: it stopped being a party led from its conservative wing, and started being one led from its liberal wing. This is significant, because the Liberal Party hasn't knowingly appointed a small-"l" liberal prime minister since 1971, when Billy McMahon took the role for a short but unhappy stint. (Malcolm Fraser, who was elected to the leadership in 1975 as a conservative, turned into much more of a liberal while in office, which is another story).

It's a fascinating development, because when the Liberal Party turfed out Malcolm Turnbull in late 2009, it was on a matter of policy – carbon pricing – which pitted climate change "believers" against climate change "sceptics." A classic left–right call of the board, with the conservative wing of the party emerging victorious.

This was a clear reinstatement of the Howard order of things. A conservative leader – Tony Abbott – installed in a clear rejection of the flashy, gay-marriage-fancying, Prius-driving outsider some in the party always suspected Malcolm Turnbull of being.

Which makes it all the more interesting that when the next leadership change happened – Tony Abbott rejected and Malcolm Turnbull reinstalled – the trigger factor was all about personality and nothing at all to do with ideology. The dysfunctionality of Tony Abbott's office, his inability to learn from mistakes; these were personal shortcomings for which Abbott was punished, not ideological ones. This assessment was not one exclusive to the liberal wing of the party: a chunk of the right wing moved too, their inability to bear what was going on overpowering their natural sympathy for Abbott. One of the prime drivers of the coup against Abbott, for instance – Victorian senator Mitch Fifield – was a right-winger who six years previously had helped to initiate the coup against Turnbull. Another right-wing Victorian senator – Scott Ryan – had clashed bitterly with Turnbull in 2009 but became an influential backer in 2015 and now is a close adviser.

The result is quite a fascinating structural change: a split of the party's senior right wing into Abbott loyalists on one side (Abbott himself, plus former ministers Eric Abetz and Kevin Andrews) and pragmatists on the other, like immigration minister Peter

Dutton, finance minister Mathias Cormann, social services minister Christian Porter and resources minister Josh Frydenberg, who voted for Abbott but are happy to work with Turnbull.

Turnbull does not want to goad the first group, or estrange the second. For a party of the right governed by a man of the centre, there is always the risk of someone else turning up to occupy the conservative space.

James McGrath, a Turnbull intimate and director of the coup against Abbott, and now Assistant Minister to the Prime Minister, offers this assistance: "John Howard governed the party room from the conservative wing, with one eye on the liberal wing. Malcolm Turnbull needs to govern our party from the liberal wing, with one eye on the conservative wing."

Turnbull's values, says George Brandis, are obvious. "What he says about Australia being an innovative, agile nation is what he wants. He wants to recreate Australia in his own image, like all prime ministers. For John Howard, it was the white picket fence. For Malcolm, it's about being a smart, savvy and technologically proficient nation with a vibrant services sector."

It's not – for the Liberal Party – a vision without danger. "The danger is that Malcolm is about ten to fifteen years ahead of where Australia is at. That's the danger of him," says a conservatively minded minister. "He gets where the economy needs to go. He gets that we can't just be a hole in the ground or a sheep paddock. He gets where we need to be socially – gay marriage, for example. But he needs to be aware that our party is a conservative party."

When you discuss Malcolm Turnbull with his colleagues – and this happens when you discuss any prime minister, pretty much – sooner or later they all attempt a comparison with one of his predecessors in office.

Politics is such a strange business that most of the time, in order to define themselves or evaluate a colleague, politicians can only ever invoke comparisons with other politicians. You never hear them say: "He reminds me of Steve Jobs," or "That was a Packerstyle manoeuvre." Politics is different from just about every other sort of enterprise, which goes some way towards explaining why Malcolm Turnbull is such a different kind of politician.

Even for the hardy band of "Which Prime Minister Is That?" spotters in the Liberal Party, Turnbull defies obvious categorisation.

"He's a contemporary Menzian Liberal," offers one minister.

"He's got an activist view of government. That's where the comparison with Deakin is quite apt," says another.

A third minister gives a potted history. "You've got Menzies, who was socially conservative and economically liberal. Then you've got Fraser, who was socially quite liberal but economically conservative. Howard: socially conservative, economically liberal. Tony Abbott, socially conservative and economically ... who knows? And now Malcolm, who is socially liberal and economically liberal."

The Deakin-comparer comes back with another analysis which surely would get him beaten up round at Menzies House. "He is that oxymoronic thing: an economically literate Whitlamite."

The gist of it seems to be that Turnbull is modern. That he is for freedom in all its forms, whether applied to the operation of markets or to the decisions people make about their own lives. But that he is not suspicious of the state in the way some of his colleagues are. He believes in state institutions and their capacity to do good.

There are a few prime ministers whose legacies are squabbled over in the Liberal Party. One – the most obvious – is Menzies. John Howard placed dibs on Menzies by writing a long biography of him in 2014, and Cory Bernardi – the right-wing South Australian senator currently tinkering about with a new conservative movement – recently declared: "It's time Australian conservatives reclaimed Menzies' vision."

"I nearly fell off my chair when I heard that!" says a

senior Liberal moderate, who points out that Menzies was less of a social conservative than John Howard.

Alfred Deakin – Australia's second prime minister – is another Liberal after whom other Liberals like to fashion themselves. This is usually accomplished by giving an Alfred Deakin Lecture in which they pummel their opponents, as did George Brandis in 2009, when he argued that John Howard had – in office – precisely inverted the Deakinite tradition, which was one of social liberalism and economic conservatism. Or Malcolm Turnbull, who in 2012 used his Alfred Deakin Lecture – in part – to express his "very grave misgivings" about the Gillard government's proposal for the compulsory retention of metadata. (Tragically, these were reforms that Turnbull and Brandis were – just two years later – obliged themselves to undertake as part of the Abbott cabinet. Another year on, and Malcolm Turnbull would be the prime minister who presided over their formal introduction.)

I started idly reading about Deakin – about whom I didn't know very much – when I worked out that he and Malcolm Turnbull were the only two Australian prime ministers who had worked both as barristers and as journalists before going into politics. The further I read, the stranger the synchronicities that emerged between their lives, which were lived nearly a century apart.

Deakin was born in 1856, Turnbull ninety-eight years later, in 1954. Both grew up ferociously interested in reading, and both were debaters at university, where they both studied law. Where Turnbull wrote competent undergraduate poetry and noodled around on ambitious musicals with Bob Ellis, Deakin wrote and published a five-act play when he was eighteen, based upon the life of the Flemish painter Quentin Matsys.

One thing the two men do not have in common was that as a teenager and young man Alfred Deakin was a committed spiritualist. He edited a spiritualist newspaper at the University of Melbourne and participated in regular séances during which he – over time – became convinced that he was in direct touch with John Bunyan, the seventeenth-century tinker who wrote *The Pilgrim's Progress*, one of the most-reprinted Christian works of literature in human history.

Guided directly by the spirit of Bunyan, Deakin wrote – at age twenty-two – a modern adaptation of Bunyan's famous work, called *A New Pilgrim's Progress*, whose protagonist – a man called Restless – found truth and meaning through vegetarianism. Deakin himself was a vegetarian for much of his life.

As a journalist, Malcolm Turnbull wrote for the *Bulletin*. Deakin wrote for the *Age*.

Malcolm Turnbull was thirty-three when – as a lawyer – he took on the government of Margaret

Thatcher in the *Spycatcher* case. Alfred Deakin was thirty-one when – as a state MP and leader of Victoria's delegation to the Imperial Conference in London – he buttonholed the British prime minister Lord Salisbury on the question of colonial interest in the New Hebrides.

Deakin would defy Britain again in 1908, as prime minister, when – as a passionate advocate of an independent defence identity for Australia – he approached President Roosevelt directly to bring the Great White Fleet to Australia, against the wishes of the British government.

Both men nearly ended their own political lives in acts of quasi-suicidal martyrdom. For Deakin, it came during his maiden speech to Victorian parliament, to which he had been elected at age twenty-three to be the representative for West Bourke. An irregularity was discovered after the ballot, and Deakin concluded his maiden speech – to the surprise of all around him – by resigning from office. But his career – like Turnbull's, after his "suicide by ETS" in 2009 – recovered. Deakin was elected uncontroversially at his third attempt, and served ten years in the state legislature before resigning to enter federal politics as Australia's first attorney-general.

Deakin's first stab at federal leadership was a miserable failure. His first term as prime minister lasted only 216 days; he was juggling protectionist, free-trade and Labour advocates in the parliament and described the experience as "three elevens trying to play in the same cricket match." His second was much happier, and various Australian public institutions were established on his watch: the bureaus of Census and Meteorology, the *Representation Act*, the *Copyright Act*, the *Quarantine Act* and the *Invalid and Old-Age Pensions Act*. He was a protectionist by belief, and a strong supporter of the White Australia policy; this is a part of his legacy over which modern Liberals do not squabble.

In Deakin's polymath tendencies and love of literature ("What a delight ... to pause before well-filled bookshelves in an hour of absolute leisure, and without any sense of duty to direct the lingering choice," he enthused in his diary), there is a clear parallel with Australia's twenty-ninth prime minister.

And Deakin's practice – throughout his entire prime ministerial career – of writing a pseudonymous column on Australian politics for London's *Morning Post*, a column he had his wife or daughter mail each week to preserve his identity, and in which he would routinely criticise his own decisions, sounds *exactly* like the sort of thing Malcolm Turnbull would do.

But by far the most enduring passion Deakin had, in policy terms, was for water and irrigation. It's an obsession that reaches across a century, one prime minister to another.

Deakin chaired a royal commission into irrigation in 1884, and led an expedition to California late that year to investigate water conservation schemes. Malcolm Turnbull, as a backbencher, travelled to Israel to investigate water recycling. The following year, Turnbull was appointed parliamentary secretary for water by John Howard – his first significant federal job.

It's an assignment that Turnbull remembers with much enthusiasm. "I had a good stump talk which I illustrated with slides. Which began with a magnificent Roman aqueduct and I used it to explain the water system of Rome and I tell you, it was … people were so into it. People are fascinated by water."

Fired by my new theory that Turnbull and Deakin might be, if not connected through some kind of paranormal activity, at least weirdly similar people, I telephoned Tom Harley, who is an influential Melbourne moderate prince of the Liberal Party, a friend of Turnbull's, and the great-grandson of Alfred Deakin himself.

Harley – who has inherited much of his great-grandfather's notorious charm – nonetheless was guarded. I had the strong impression he might be over people ringing him with wild theories about his ancestor.

Harley allowed that there were certain similarities. But the one he pointed out was one that hadn't occurred to me.

"The thing that people miss in all the descriptions of Deakin is that he had a vision," said Harley. "He wanted to pick the best bits of the old world and build the kind of society that he wanted to live in. I think Malcolm's in that kind of category. Federation is a dull debate because it's all about constitutional drafts and so on. But what underpinned it was that people wanted to build a marvellous new country. Malcolm's got an idea of what the future looks like. He's unremittingly positive. He has a big view of Australia based as much on deep values as it is on economic objectives and – like Deakin – he's drawing on all these sinews to create it."

I thought, as we hung up, of a story Turnbull's old press secretary Tony Barry once told me fondly about his boss. The two of them were humming along in Turnbull's Prius – a hybrid electric car of which the then Opposition leader was, naturally, an early adopter. "The thing is," said Turnbull, conversationally, "I'm either ahead of my time, or behind it. I just don't know which."

Sources

2–3   "I remember one day": Malcolm Turnbull, extended
       transcript for *Kitchen Cabinet*, ABC TV, 2013.

10   "Abbott testifies": Tony Abbott, *Kitchen Cabinet*, ABC
       TV, 4 September 2013.

13   "I must say": Turnbull, interview with Fran Kelly, ABC
       Radio National, 31 March 2016, www.pm.gov.au/
       media/2016-03-31/interview-fran-kelly-abc-rn-breakfast.

16   "a wonderful 2015 article": Alex Ellinghausen, "Finding the
       Thing: Photographing Malcolm Turnbull, Tony Abbott,
       Bill Shorten", *Sydney Morning Herald*, 11 December 2015.

17   "no 'tech head'": Abbott, interview with Kerry O'Brien,
       The 7:30 Report, ABC, 10 August 2010, www.abc.net.
       au/7.30/content/2010/s2979381.htm.

26–7   "There has never been": Malcolm Turnbull and Julie
       Bishop, press conference, Canberra, 14 September 2015,
       www.malcolmturnbull.com.au/media/transcript-vote-on-
       the-liberal-party-leadership.

27   "Labor complained": Dan Conifer, "Federal Labor Refers
       'Exciting Time' Phrase in Government Ad Campaign to
       Auditor-General", *AM*, ABC Radio, 16 March 2016,
       www.abc.net.au/am/content/2016/s4425750.htm.

32   "*Showboat* regrettably": Turnbull, extended transcript,
       Kitchen Cabinet, 2013.

33–4   "Lucille Iremonger, whose study": Lucille Iremonger, *The
       Fiery Chariot*, Martin Secker & Warburg, 1970.

34   "Malcolm Gladwell, in": Malcolm Gladwell, *David and Goliath: Underdogs, Misfits, and the Art of Battling Giants*, Little, Brown and Company, 2013.

34   "If I look back": Malcolm Turnbull, *Australian Story*, ABC TV, transcript, 3 August 2009.

35   "Look, Coral was": Turnbull, extended transcript, *Kitchen Cabinet*, 2013.

38   "Initiated by Turnbull!": Graham Richardson, "The Man Who Would Be King", *Bulletin*, 28 October 2003, p. 30.

41   "When Malcolm Turnbull": Peter Hartcher, "Brilliant and Fearless but Paul Keating Was Right About Turnbull", *Sydney Morning Herald*, 27 June 2009, www.smh.com.au/federal-politics/brilliant-and-fearless-but-paul-keating-was-right-about-turnbull-20090626-czt7.html.

41–2   "I think we have": Turnbull, interview with Karen Barlow, *The World Today*, 28 May 2008, www.abc.net.au/worldtoday/content/2008/s2258063.htm

45   "I was fairly": John Howard, in Patrick O'Brien, *The Liberals: Factions, Feuds and Fancies*, Viking: Melbourne, 1985, p. 84.

46   "a leftish weekly called *Nation Review*": Malcolm Turnbull, *The Spycatcher Trial*, Heinemann Australia: Melbourne, 1988, p. 2.

46   "I was serving, simultaneously, Marx, God and Mammon": Turnbull, *The Spycatcher Trial*, p. 2.

46–7   "Tony Abbott … promptly organised a pro-Kerr rally": Michael Duffy, *Latham and Abbott*, Random House: Sydney, 2004, p. 34.

52   "For all his firebrand ways": Mark Latham, "The Forgotten Land", *The Hummer*, publication of the Sydney Branch, Australian Society for the Study of Labour History, April–August 1992, p. 121.

52   "What it was that drew them": Bob Ellis, "An Honourable, Fidgetty, Humanist Liberalism", ABC *Unleashed*,

3 December 2007, www.abc.net.au/unleashed/stories/
s2107621.htm.

53–4   "If Lang's depression politics": Malcolm Turnbull, "Lang: A Man Who Knew How to Hate", *Nation Review*, 3–9 October 1975, p. 1299.

58   "the unbowdlerised account": Conrad Black, *A Life In Progress*, Key Porter Books, Toronto, 1993, p. 436.

58   "It showed Turnbull": Alan Ramsey, "Malcolm, The Mogul and Moggy Myths", *Sydney Morning Herald*, 20 September 2008.

59   "Malcolm is really a pussycat": Phillip Adams in John Lyons, "Raging Turnbull", *Good Weekend*, 13 April 1991, p. 21.

60   "He's a turd": McClelland in Lyons, "Raging Turnbull".

60   "a bitter old man": Turnbull in Lyons, "Raging Turnbull".

64–5   "One has to be" etc.: Malcolm Turnbull, "Gough Whitlam", *Honi Soit*, 26, 1974, p. 5.

72   "Lavish detail": Peter Hartcher, "Tony Abbott Rolled by His Own Ministers over Stripping Terrorists of Citizenship", *Sydney Morning Herald*, 29 May 2015.

72   "The greatest tragedy": Malcolm Turnbull, "Magna Carta and the Rule of Law in the Digital Age", speech to the Sydney Institute, 7 July 2015.

78   "The Turnbull-ARM republic": Ross Cameron, *Hansard*, 30 August 1999, p. 57.

81   "Tackling Costigan": Turnbull, *The Spycatcher Trial*, p. 7.

87–8   "The quality of these conversations": Turnbull, *The Spycatcher Trial*, p. 15.

88–90   "We need to get Peter" and "'In order to flush out'": Turnbull, *The Spycatcher Trial*, p. 27–8, 117.

92   "All conflicts can be resolved": Turnbull, interview with Marian Wilkinson and Paul Syvret, *Sydney Morning Herald*, 22 September 1990.

92   "It's all a question": Turnbull in John Sampson, "Media Casualty", *Age*, 23 September 1990.

93   "It is refreshing": Malcolm Turnbull, "The Law", *Bulletin*, 14 July 1981.

93   "Mum's next book": Coral Lansbury, *The Old Brown Dog: Women, Workers and Vivisection in Edwardian England*, University of Wisconsin Press, 1985.

98   "Sitting back and watching": Colleen Ryan and Glenn Burge, *Corporate Cannibals: The Taking Of Fairfax*, Mandarin Australia, Melbourne, 1993, p. 74.

99   "best defined as": Malcolm Turnbull, "PM's Cheap Money Shot", *Weekend Australian*, 7–8 March 2009.

100   "People have always had": Suellen O'Grady, "What Malcolm Wants, Malcolm Gets", *Good Weekend*, 3 September 1988, p. 60.

106   "an intelligent, attractive and articulate man": Black, *A Life in Progress* p. 436.

108   "No judge is ever": O'Grady, "What Malcolm Wants, Malcolm Gets", p. 60.

113   "One dark winter afternoon": Charles Moore, "I Don't Want Your Cash, Mr Murdoch", *Independent*, 23 September 2003.

121   "mismanaged the ABCC bill": Paul Kelly, "Malcolm Turnbull Flies High but Storms Threaten", *Australian*, 19 March 2016.

125   "What we're talking about": Malcolm Turnbull, doorstep interview, Penrith, 30 March 2016, http://malcolmturnbull.com.au/media/doorstop-penrith.

138   "In the past" etc.: Turnbull, interview with Fran Kelly, *Radio National Breakfast*, 28 November 2007.

143   "These are grave allegations": Turnbull, interview with Lyndal Curtis, *PM*, Radio National, 19 June 2009, www.abc.net.au/pm/content/2008/s2603446.htm.

143   "The prime minister and the treasurer": Malcolm Turnbull, press conference, 19 June 2009.

Sources

146–7   "not all it's cracked up to be", "I ripped off": Andrew
        Robb, *Black Dog Daze*, MUP, 2011, p. 165

148   "Malcolm can be ruthless": Robb, *Black Dog Daze*, p. 166.

149   "we will end up becoming": Turnbull to Laurie Oakes,
        Nine Network, 2009.

155   "Lucy decided" etc.: Turnbull, *Kitchen Cabinet* transcript,
        ABC TV, 2 July 2013.

170   "I am a different": Turnbull, interview with Neil Mitchell,
        3AW Melbourne, 22 March 2016, *PM*, ABC Radio,
        www.pm.gov.au/media/2016-03-22/interview-neil-mitchell-
        3aw-melbourne.

175   "Pragmatism, experience and commonsense": Turnbull,
        maiden speech, 29 October 2004, www.malcolmturnbull.
        com.au/meet-malcolm/first-speech.

175   "I am not an ideological person": Turnbull, interview with
        Fran Kelly, *Radio National Breakfast*, 28 November 2007.

180   "I fancy Malcolm": Eleanor Hall, interview with Paul
        Keating, *The World Today*, 26 November 2007.

180–1   "There are risks for everybody": Malcolm Turnbull, ABC
        News 24, 7 December 2015

181–2   "The first and most": David Kemp, "A Leader and a
        Philosophy", *Checkpoint*, vol. 13, 1973, pp. 3–13.

193   "What a delight": Al Gabay, *The Mystic Life of Alfred
        Deakin*, Cambridge University Press, 1992 p. 41.